MW01490476

This book is dedicated to my children, Christopher, Samantha, Matthew, and Tiffany. My grandchildren Aisly, and Levi. I pray that you all live a happy and fulfilling life. Do not be afraid to take chances, love with all your heart, and never give up hope. Things happen in life that we do not always understand. Our life is a journey: there will be pain, hurt, confusion, trials, sadness, joy, and happiness that you will experience throughout life. Every day God gives you another breath, he gives you another day to have influence, change old habits, situations, jobs, relationships, or whatever you need. Always remember your story is not over, no matter what the situation is, there is always another day to try again. To my mother, I am glad you are in my life. To my father, rest in peace. To my sister, I pray you find healing. To all those who encouraged me, and to all the people I have hurt along the way. A special Thank you to Pastor Chad, Pastor Ivory, Vess and Michelle for all you have done. You all have shown me love, kindness, and compassion that I will never forget. You all hold a special place in my heart and have been a great inspiration in my life. I want you to know that I will always love you.

Chapter 1

My childhood was not ideal for a young child. Certain events occurred that no child should ever have to experience. I was four years old when my father left home. My father cheated on my mother on several occasions. He was not an incredibly good father or husband, so my mother made him leave. Even though they had problems, I never understood why she kept him from our lives over the years. In her own way, she had her reason. I guess.

After my father left home, my mother developed another unhealthy relationship with another man. I can still remember the day when I asked her who he was. "This is your new daddy." Mom replied. I have never forgotten those words. I am not sure what my mother was thinking when she got with him because he was a wicked man. He started to abuse my mother and sexually abused my sister and me. He had abused my mother so badly that he almost killed her. The things he made us do are unspeakable. I did not remember much about my father then but surely it was not as bad as this guy.

The trauma I experienced during this time made me feel dirty, unloved, ashamed, and ugly. Here, I was a young child, and this man had violated my body. I was around five or six when it all started. I blocked so much out but there are some memories that never left me. This is where those thoughts about me started to develop. I was a bad child, no-one could love me, no-one would want me, and no-one cared. My mother could not even stop this from happening. Why was this happening and why can't anyone make him stop?

My father was not around, he had no idea what was going on. I can still remember a time; I heard my father; outside driving around saying, "I will find my girls someday." I do not know whether it really happened, or if it was just a dream. I waited so long for my father to come and rescue me. Every night I would pray for my daddy to save me, to protect me, to love me, to want me. *"Resue me from my enemies, LORD, for I hide myself in you."* Psalms 143:9 NIV.

Prayer-

Dear Heavenly Father,

Please send my daddy to save me. In Jesus name I pray. Amen

The abuse continued, and nothing ever seemed to change. My mother and her boyfriend were alcoholics and did not care much about what was going on around them. I never understood as to why she let it continue. Why was she not strong enough to leave? *"Be strong and courageous. Do not be afraid or terrified because of them, for the Lord your God goes with you: he will never leave you nor forsake you. "Deuteronomy 31:6 NIV.* Why did she continue to let this man hurt her children, hurt her? Was she afraid? Whenever I am afraid, I put my trust in the LORD. *"When I am afraid, I put my trust and faith in you" Psalm 56:3 AMP.* If only my mother knew God, or did she?

My mother was not an affectionate kind of person, so I can only assume it was how she was raised. Her upbringings were different in the fifties. She grew up in a Methodist Church, so she knew about God. My grandfather was the kind of man that listened to gossip music but was an acholic. He was extremely strict. The girls were only allowed to wear dresses. When they were in trouble, they were spanked with a razor strap. He would always accuse the girls of messing around with boys in the halls at school. My mother was one of twelve children, she was the oldest of all the girls.

My mother never experienced a healthy kind of love from her parents. When my grandparents divorced, my grandfather called social services on my grandmother. They stated my grandmother had too many children to care for on her own. All the younger children were adopted to other families. My grandmother died at the age of forty-two. My mother was in her early twenties when my grandmother passed away. I never had the opportunity to meet her, but I was told I resemble her.

Over the years, our family had told me that my mother would leave that horrible man, but he always found her. Of course, she always went back to him because I do not remember her ever leaving but one time. My sister and I told her a number of times that we were tired of her boyfriend doing those things to us. She had to make it stop or we were going to run away. *"When the righteous cry {for help} the LORD hears AND rescues them from all their distress and troubles." Psalm 34:17 AMP.*

The time I do remember my mother leaving, she had stayed with some friends of hers. I was around ten or eleven years old by this time, maybe younger. This friend, well she had a teenage daughter who had a boyfriend. Her boyfriend sexual assaulted me more than once. I never told anyone, well because I was afraid. Who would believe me, my mother? She did not even stop what her boyfriend was doing to my sister and me. I thought this was my fault. Was there something about me that made men do these things to me? I did not understand why my mother just could not protect me from all the terrible things that kept happening.

I can still remember so many of these sexual encounters as if it were a horror movie playing in my head. Two men had violated my body, who made me feel so ashamed of myself. Over time I would just stay in my room, sitting in the corner of my bed, just crying. Hoping and praying that my father would find me and save me. I did not know much about God back then. If I did, maybe he could have saved me.

Was God even real? if so than why would he let terrible things happen to people, to children? As I grew up, I honestly believed that God only created woman to satisfy man. The bible does say God created woman for man. Was God good or evil? *"The LORD God said, "It is not good for the man to be alone. I will make a helper suitable for him." Genesis 2:18 NIV.* It is not of God for such things to happen to us. If it is not of love, it is not God. God is Good. *"Whoever does not love does not know God, because God is love." 1 John 4:8 NIV.* I had no good examples in my life, so I was not sure what to believe. My parents were supposed to protect me, love me, and comfort me whenever terrible things happened.

The older I got the more the memories started to fade but the scars remain. "My past will never define me, only my further." I have told myself this repeatedly. The agony I have felt over the years all started from this man who sexually assaulted me when I was so young. That man took my childhood, my womanhood, respect for myself, my teenage life, and so much more. God has delivered me from so much pain in my life. *"Keep me safe, Lord, from the hands of the wicked." Psalms 140:4 NIV. "but whoever listens to me will live in safety and be at ease, without fear of harm." Proverbs 1:33 NIV.*

For several years, I placed the blame on other people for how my life turned out. I always keep making mistakes, getting myself in the wrong situations, feeling sorry for myself, thinking I was not worthy of love. *"No one should accuse or blame another person" Hosea 4:4 NIV.* I never understood how a parent could let someone hurt their children. Then I grew up and started repeating unhealthy relationships. I lived my life in darkness, it was what I knew. I did not have the perfect role models in my life. I had no-one to look up to. Chaos and disaster were normal in my life. *"In all your ways know and acknowledge and recognize Him, And he will make your paths straight and smooth {removing obstacles that block your way} Proverbs 3:6 AMP.*

When I talk about relationships, I am referring to various kinds of relationships, not just intimate relationships. You have friendships, relationships with co-workers, family members, boyfriends/girlfriends. I am clarifying those relationships because in my experience there have always been people out there that automatically assumes an intimate relationship. We encounter relationships in everyday life even when you do not realize it. *"Have the same attitude in yourselves which was in Christ Jesus* *{look to Him as your example in selfless humility} Philippians 2:5 AMP.*

Twenty-five years ago, I started writing a book titled "Shattered Dreams," although it remains incomplete to this day. I wanted to write about my story to inform other teenage girls about young motherhood. As time passed there were more events that happened in my life. It seemed as If I would never get to the end. I wanted to find a happy ending to my story. I kept waiting and waiting and nothing seemed to change. It was one disaster after another. Today, I want to tell you how God changed my life. We have two choices, let the past define you and continue the same journey, or change your future through the eyes of the Lord. *"For I know the plans and thoughts that I have for you, says the LORD, 'plans for peace and well-being and not for disaster, to give you a future and a hope" Jeremiah 29:11 AMP.* Our happiness lies in our hands. We determine our destiny not our circumstances. Do not force something if it does not fit and pray to God to direct us on the right path.

Twelve years ago, someone came into my life. He talked about God a lot. Every bible verse he told me or how he praised God. I wanted to know more. I wanted to know about that God, not the God I had imagined in my mind over the years. I always believed God was real, but I did not understand why he did not stop horrible things in this messed up world. Never in my life have I heard someone talk about God the way he did. I believe that he came into my life for a reason not a season. I hope you find courage, hope, faith, peace, and love. God has shown me miracles; he has always provided for me and my family. Whenever one door closed, God opened another door of opportunities. All I had to do was believe. *"Ask, and it will be given to you: seek, and you will find; knock and the door will be opened to you." Mathew 7:7 NIV*

Everything that I went through as a child, a teenager, a mother, and a wife. God changed me, my way of thinking, everything I use to feel. "My past will never define me, only my further." This quote has helped me to keep pushing through. *"Therefore, if anyone is in Christ, the new creation has come. The old has gone, and the new is here."* 2 Corinthians 5:17 NIV. God loves me, forgives me, and will never forsake me. I believe what the Lord says about me. " I am rooted in the Lord, and I will survive." I waited so much of my life waiting for that miracle, to have happiness in my life. All along it was God who held the key to my victory. *"And now these three remain: faith, hope, and love. But the greatest of these is love."* 1 Corinthians 13:13 NIV.

God was just waiting for me to accept him in my heart, to ask him for forgiveness for the mistakes I had made. To accept him, as my Lord and Savior and I would be saved. I had to forgive those that hurt me, those that betrayed me, abused me, lied to me, deceived me, and those who stole from me. Some may say "Why should I forgive; they did not ask for forgiveness? or God does not expect you to forgive if they did not ask for forgiveness. *For if you forgive other people when they sin against you, your heavenly Father will also forgive you"* Matthew 6:14 NIV. Many people decide they cannot forgive. It is too hard, so they refuse. Forgiving someone is extremely difficult but not forgiving is a mistake. If we do not forgive, it interferes with our intimacy with God.

Well, I am here to tell you, my friends. Regardless of what others say about forgiveness. Holding on to those burdens, hatred, bitterness, you cannot find joy or happiness in life. *"Bearing graciously with one another, and willingly forgiving each other if one has a cause for complaint against another, just as the LORD has forgiven you, so should you forgive."* Colossians 3:13 AMP. Even though we forgive, it does not mean you have to have a relationship with that person. You can pray and love them from a distance. *"But I tell you, love your enemies and pray for those who persecute you."* Matthew 5:44 NIV.

Now, I have told you where it all began and about my faith to God. God has pulled me from toxic relationships that where in my life. My life has been a journey. There were good times along with difficult times. The more I started to believe God's words about me, focusing on God and God alone, the happier I was. *"Be kind and compassionate to one another, forgiving each other, just as in Christ God forgave you" Ephesians 4:32 NIV.* I found peace, joy, love, happiness, grace and forgiveness within God.

Prayer-

Dear Heavenly Father,

I know that releasing forgiveness is important. Help me to forgive those who have hurt me, to forgive myself for my choices, and give me the strength to stand firm, knowing your love supports me. In Jesus name I pray. Amen

When we let fear into our lives, it takes control. When you allow people's negative words to take control of our minds, it makes us weak. *"And he said unto me, 'My grace for thee: for my strength is made perfect in weakness, when you allow your mind to take control of the negative things around you are weak. "Submit yourselves therefore to God. Resist the devil, and he will flee from you." 2 Corinthians 12:9 NIV & James 4:7 NIV.* This bible verse talks about the power of God's grace working through our weakness. It is also important to resist negative influence by submitting to God's authority. If we follow the word of God, he has the strength to renew our hearts and our minds that will allow us to have a brighter future. If you believe, you will receive.

I lacked love from others around me. During that time in my life, I felt so alone, afraid, lost, confused, and sad. I needed my parents more than they realized. Now I know all I needed was God's love. I just needed to reach for God to provide guidance, strength, love, grace, and forgiveness. Today, whenever those emotions start to roll through my body, like a washing machine at full speed. My emotions start to take over. I must stop, get in the word of God. Rinse and repeat. Meaning, stay in the word of God, and do not loss side of that. God is my strength.

I did not really know the definition of love. *"Love is patient, Love is Kind. It does not envy, it does not boast, it is not proud."* 1 Corinthians 13:4 NIV. During those years of the abuse, my mother turned to alcohol. I believe it was her way of dealing with the demons inside of her. *"Through my father and mother forsake me, the Lord will receive me, teach me your way, Lord: lead me in a straight path because of my oppressors."* Psalm 27:10-11 NIV. I still struggle with people that suffer from addictions. I know they have their own battles to fight. For me, it still brings painful memories.

I have forgiven my mother for the trauma she allowed to happen in my life. We do have a wonderful relationship today. She is my best friend, and my mother. If I had held onto that bitterness, anger, resentment, hatred, and confusion. We would not have a relationship today. *"For God is not a God of confusion, but of peace."* 1 Corinthians 14:33 ESV. *"Get rid of all bittiness, rage, and anger, brawling, and slander, along with every form of malice."* Ephesians 4:31 NIV. We are always there for each other. She may not have protected me back then, but she loves me today. She asked God for forgiveness, and is working to change her ways in the eyes of the Lord.

I have forgiven my father for the mistakes he has made, and for leaving me. Our relationship was rocky for several years, until he found out I graduated from college. My father should have loved and cared for me regardless of the choices I made. I did not agree with my father's choices, or the way he treated people. We cannot change people to be who we think they should be. We can only pray for them. Accept them for who they are, we all have flaws, we are all broken. We need to love them just like Christ Jesus. *"What, then, shall we say in response to these things? If God is for us, who can be against us? Romans 8:31 NIV.* Over time, we were able to put the past behind us, set aside our differences and build a healthy relationship. I am truly thankful and blessed that I did because I got that time with my father before he passed away. It is all because of God.

Prayer-

Dear Heavenly Father,

Thank you for all you have done in my life. Thank you for giving me the strength to rebuild a relationship with my parents. I am so grateful for everything you do in my life. Thank you for loving me, and giving me comfort every time my heart is aching. Thank you for giving me another breath. I pray that you continue to give me courage, strength, and the tools I need to show people love even when it is hard. In Jesus name I pray. Amen

Chapter 2

The day had finally come, my mother was brave, courageous, strong, and determined. *"Have I not commanded you? Be strong and courageous. Do not be afraid; do not be discouraged, for the LORD your God will be with you whenever you go." Joshua 1:9 NIV.* She had planned her escape; she was going to take us away from that wicked man. She quit drinking and focused on our new beginning. I was around twelve years old by then. She got a job working at a nursing home and decided to finish pursuing her nursing career. She was attending nursing school back when she was with my father. Life happened, and she stopped.

God was giving her the strength she needed to remove the toxic relationship in her life. *"He gives strength to the weary and increases the power of the weak." Isaiah 40:29 NIV.* A moment in her life she had to be brave, for her daughters but mostly for herself. I was so proud of my mother for taking a leap of faith, to remove us from this tragic environment. *"May the Lord now show you kindness and faithfulness, and I too will show you the same favor because you have done this." 2 Samuel 2:6 NIV.* She was going to give her daughters a better life, to protect them, love them, and guide them. Instead of filling our mind with the negative traumas that happen in our life's. Fill them with God's word. It has helped me tremendously.

We got an apartment in a small town, Harrisonville, Missouri. It was a yellow duplex with black shutters. It was right next to the city park, within walking distance. Our mother would be working nights, so she was not home much with us. My sister and I went to school, did our chores, and homework. After all that was done mom would let us do whatever we wanted. We were not allowed to have friends over if mom was not home. We had a curfew, and we had to stay out of trouble. Most of the time, my sister and I loved to walk to the park or sit outside on the porch and watch the cars drive by.

There were times we were still hoping that one day our father would find us. It had been eight years by now, and nothing. We did not trust our mother to keep us safe. *"In spite of this, you did not trust in the Lord your God." Deuteronomy 1:32 NIV.* All we had was a little hope and a little faith. My sister and I used to pray over the years, but we started to lose that faith. Maybe, just maybe God had finally answered our prayers. *"He replied, "Because you have so little faith. Truly I tell you, if you have faith as small as a mustard seed, you can say to this mountain, 'Move from here to there,' and it will move. Nothing will be impossible for you." Matthew 17:20 NIV.*

My sister and I started going to a Baptist church in Harrisonville. We really loved it, until the church changed. The building had been built shaped like an ARC, it was unique. One day we attended, and people were rolling around on the floor. We had no idea what they were doing, so we stopped going. Now I know, they were worshiping God. Some people praise and worship God differently. *"God is spirit, and his worshipers must worship in the spirit and in truth." John 4:24 NIV.* We have never experienced religion in our years of growing up, so we had no idea.

Our lives were getting better, my sister and I started to feel safe. Mom was working every day and was becoming an RN (registered nurse). We still did not see her much; my sister and I became inseparable. We did everything together. We loved our new place. We would sit outside on the porch every chance we got and take walks to the park. We finally had freedom. We were safe and secure; we were finally happy. Our mother was really trying this time. We were never to speak of what had happened. Our mother was afraid, afraid of us being taken away. *" So then, don't be afraid. I will provide for you and your children." And he reassured them and spoke kindly to them. Genesis 50:21 NIV.*

I remember one day we had walked to the city park and there were these boys' playing tennis. There was one boy who caught my attention, but I was not about to introduce myself. I thought he was so cute. My sister, yells out saying "My sister thinks your cute." I started running back home when he came after me. I was so embarrassed but glad he came to talk to me. He walked me home that day. We really liked each other. Brody was my first boyfriend. Thirty-seven years later, I can still remember our first kiss, my first kiss.

Another day, my sister and I were sitting outside on the porch watching the cars drive by, when a car stopped. The first time it stopped, my sister told him she had a boyfriend. He drove around again trying to get her attention, he was not giving up so easily. Later that night, we told our mother about what happened. The same car was driving down the road at that moment. Now, that was a coincidence. My mother walks outside and yells out to them "Do you want to party?" She was just messing around with them. However, they did not take it as that. Well, you can only imagine what happened next. There were a couple of guys in the car, one of them that really liked my sister. Of course, this time my sister is single as she tells him.

His name was Cameron. He keeps coming around wanting her more. One night he showed up and my sister's boyfriend was there. He brought a beautiful red rose with him. My sister totally ignored Cameron but finally told him she was not interested. Cameron still did not leave, instead he started talking to me. He told me the rose was for me; he was just using my sister to get to me. It was foolish for me to fall into his deception. *"Watch out that no one deceives you" Matthew 24:4 NIV.* I was thirteen years old, around this time. A gullible girl looking for love. He gave me attention, and my heart swam for his affection.

About a week later I broke it off with Brody. This is the first time in my existence; I felt like I was unworthy. Brody came from a good family. If he knew what happened to me previously. He probably would have run. I felt like I was dirty, unworthy, and was ashamed of who I was. *"Forget the former things; do not dwell on the past. Isaiah 43:18 NIV.* He deserved so much more than a girl like me. That was my way of thinking. If he knew that I was not a virgin, and why. How could I explain myself? I was not allowed to tell anyone. It was not a chance I was willing to take. He deserved so much more than a girl like me.

We should not have self-doubt about ourselves. It is especially important to learn to love who you are. You may not have the best of background, but God made you in his image. God loves you and he knows who you are. We are worthy, we are worthy of good things, we are worthy of love. I have to consistently tell myself this, because sometimes my past makes me believe otherwise. As scripture says, *"Anyone who believes in him will never be put to shame." Romans 10:11 NIV.* But be careful because the enemy wants you to believe your unworthy, so you go back and follow his ways.

I have thought about Brody so much over the years. I always hoped he had a good life, a good wife, and started a family. I tried to find him over the years but what would I say? Several years ago, I tried to send a letter to apologize but I never knew if it reached him. I do not even think he would remember me after all these years. The last time I knew he had moved away, got married and had two children. He is one good thing that was in my life that I never forgot. So many times, I have gone back to that park, thinking that is where everything in my life changed. *"Forgetting what lies behind and reaching forward to what lies ahead." Philippians 3:13 NKJV.*

Feeling regret is normal for humans to experience, but God wants us to deal with it through repentance and to seek forgiveness from God. *"So repent {change your inner self-your old way of thinking, regret past sins} and return {to God-seek His purpose for your life} so that your sins may be wiped away {blotted out, completely erased} so that times of refreshing may come from the presence of the LORD {restoring you like a cool wind on a hot day} Acts 3:19 AMP.* Trust God that he can cleanse you, so you can move forward without being burden from your past. We must admit to our weakness, failures, and mistakes to God. When we think we fall short of perfection, the enemy will consistently get into our mind, convince us that we are not worthy because of what we have done or where we have been. *"Cast all your anxiety on him because he cares for you. 1 Peter 5:7 NIV.* God says to prepare for not where you have been, not where you are, but grab ahold of something that is bigger than you.

My way of thinking and emotions was like going on the roller coaster Mamba. If you have ever experienced riding this roller coaster you will know what I mean. It goes seventy-five miles per hour. It goes up high, down low, in circles, backwards, and upside down. I did not know what to think or believe. *"Godly sorrow brings repentance that leads to salvation and leaves no regret, but worldly sorrow brings death" 2 Corinthians 7:10 NIV.* All I knew was how I felt about myself. For thirty-eight years, I felt like I was worthless, that led me straight down into darkness.

Our past can take control of our minds if we allow it to. The devil will come to kill, steal, and destroy. *"The thief comes only to steal and kill and destroy; I have come that they may have life and have it to the full." John 10:10 NIV.* Be careful with your thoughts and try to stay in the word of God. God's word is truth. No matter what we have been through, God is who will set us free from all those burdens, which weighs so heavily on our shoulders. *"I can do all this through him who gives me strength." Philippians 4:13 NIV.*

Cameron was nineteen years old; he was older than me. We started hanging out together. The more time I spent with Cameron, the more I liked him. He made me feel safe and loved. No matter how damaged I was, he accepted me for all my flaws. He was too old for me to be dating but I did anyway. Looking back today, I do not know what I had seen in him. It was the security that he gave me, I guess. All along, he was deceiving me to get to my sister. He still had an infatuation for her, but I ignored it. Recognize deception before it turns to destruction. *"Let no one deceive you with empty words, for because of such things God's wrath comes on those who are disobedient." Ephesians 5:6 NIV.*

It finally felt like we were finally free from the despicable things that happened in our lives. Until that day Wayne found us. *"Even though I walk through the {sunless} valley of the shadow of death, I fear no evil, for You are with me; Your rod {to protect} and Your staff {to guide} they comfort and console me." Psalms 23:4 AMP.* Small world but his nephew ended up moving in next door to us. One day they were talking, and the neighbor mentioned our names. I still remember Wayne's full name to this day. I blocked out a lot over the years, but I never forgot the names of the men who sexually assaulted me.

Someone was knocking on the door and my mother answered. It was Wayne, she was so frightened when she saw him at the door. *"The Lord is my helper {in time of need} I will not be afraid. What will man do to me? Hebrews 13:6 AMP.* She told him he had better leave before she called the police. He did not listen; he shoved her out of the way and forced himself into our home. His nephew and his wife were there visiting. Wayne, stumbling through the house goes straight to the couch and sits down next to his nephew.

My mother went to sit in her chair. She had one of those recliners and there was an end table that sat right next to it. There was a little lamp that sat on the table. If I closed my eyes and just thought about that moment, I could remember that image as if it were just yesterday. I do not remember a lot, between that moment and when the police arrived. Some of the memories are a blur, but some still remain. That day was the end of it all.

Wayne sat there, talking about everything. He admitted everything he did to my sister and me. How the sex was, and words I cannot even repeat. Those words have never left me. There are things that happen in our lives that sometimes we block out. There are some things that just never leave our mind. Well, that was one of them. I can still remember things he said that have tormented me my whole life. Until the day I allowed God into my heart. *"As well as those who were tormented with unclean spirits. And they were healed. Luke 6:18 NKJV.* The scars will always remain; however, Wayne no longer has power over my mind, spirit, and soul.

My mother kept telling him to leave, but he refused. He got up from the couch and started to charge after my mother. He grabbed the lamp that was sitting next to her. As he was about to hit her over the head with it. His nephew stepped in to stop him. My sister runs outside to Wayne's truck to grab the gun. He always kept a rifle that hung in the back window of his pickup truck. I do not remember this part of it, but my sister does. *"The Lord tests the righteous and the wicked, And His soul hates the {malevolent} one who loves violence." Psalm 11:5 AMP.*

The police officers finally showed up and my mother told them everything. Well, I assume she did, someone did. Wayne went to jail and was placed on a twenty-four-hour hold. He was released but was not charged for sexual assault or the assault towards my mother. He was drunk, so he was considered incompetent. He admitted everything that night, but it meant nothing. He was free out in the world, able to do it to another family. We were devastated; we were no longer safe. *"The LORD is good, A strength and stronghold in the day of trouble; He knows {He recognizes, cares for, and understands fully} those who take refuge and trust in Him." Nahum 1:7 AMP.*

We never seen Wayne again after that night, well there was possibly one more time.

I will get to that later. We started to unravel the trauma from which we just could not escape. I got closer to Cameron. When he found out what happened, he would stay overnight. He was not going to allow Wayne to ever hurt us again. That is when I started to fall in love with him. Anyways, I thought it was love. Looking back now, I just felt safe. He tried so hard to protect me. At that moment I thought that was what I needed.

Cameron and I dated for a few months before he came to tell me he was moving away. He had family in Florida and there was a job already waiting for him. He was planning to leave in a couple of weeks. I was devastated. I thought I loved him, and I could not stand the idea of him leaving me. I wanted to be with him always. Cameron did not want to leave me either; he said he loved me and wanted me to go with him. I was thirteen years old. I could not go unless my mother allowed me to.

Children should honor their parents with loving hearts of obedience, whether or not they deserve it. "Children, obey your parents in the Lord {that is, accept their guidance and discipline as His representatives} for this is right {for obedience teaches wisdom and self-discipline} Honor {esteem, value as precious} your father and your mother {and be respectful to them} this is the first commandment with a promise— so that it may be well with you, and that you may have a long life on the earth." *Ephesians 6:1-3 AMP*. Trust me, I know it can be hard. We imagine in our minds how we think our parents should be. The truth of the matter is, we cannot be everything everyone expects us to be. Parenting is hard for anyone, not alone trying to make the right choices. However, if we follow God , it is he who can direct our steps. He is the one to show us how to love those that make it difficult to love.

Chapter 3

How could I ask my mother if I could move to Florida, would she allow it? My thoughts were running wild. My heart was palpitating, and tears were falling. Cameron said my family could come with me. I was still scared to ask my mother if we could move to Florida. I waited a couple of days, replaying in my head repeatedly. How would I get the courage to ask my mother if we could move to Florida?

If only I talked to her before Cameron. I had so many things against her that I could use to get her to say yes. *"Honor (respect, obey, care for) your father and your mother, so that your days may be prolonged in the land the LORD gave you." Exodus 20:12 AMP.* Wayne had already found us, so I had that. I was also in love with Cameron, anyways I thought I was. I could not imagine my life without him. Cameron was a scruffy kind of guy, with dishwater blonde hair. He never brushed his hair and always wore a hat. He would say that is what the hat was for. He was about five feet eleven inches tall, big built, strong, and muscular. Looking back on those memories, the biggest attraction was that he made me feel safe.

One night after my mother got off work, I talked to her and my sister about their thoughts about us moving to Florida. I had negotiated my side of things. How this may be our opportunity to escape for the last time. The further away we were the harder it would be for Wayne to find us. After manipulating my mother, using every angle I could, every reason and excuse I could use. I finally got my mother to say, "Yes. I told her Cameron would be by and would discuss things in more detail. He had a plan, and it was going to work. I was sure of it.

I used those mistakes that my mother made and manipulated her to get what I wanted. There were difficulties in our lives, which is undeniable. My mother was doing great, and she was stronger than ever. She did not allow Wayne to hurt us anymore. She did the right thing by calling the police, trying to make him leave. She was standing strong. *"Honor your father and mother, and love your neighbor as yourself." Matthew 19:19 NIV.* I should not have used that against her. All I knew at the time was Cameron made me feel safe and loved. Seek and pray to God to direct us in making the right decisions. Our feelings are not facts, and our heart can and will deceive us. *"If any lacks wisdom, you should ask God, who gives generously to all without finding fault and it will be given to you." James 1:5 NIV.*

The next couple of days Cameron came by to talk things over with my mother. He told her he was going to head out to Florida first. He would be staying with family until he saved enough money to get a place of his own. When he got everything established, we were to pack everything in my mother's car and drive to Florida. We were going to stay with Cameron until my mother found a job and got a place of her own. He was leaving in just two more days. I was so excited about our new adventure. I was so sure that Cameron would not forget about me. He came into my life, and at the time I thought I needed to be rescued.

In my world, it was like an escape from the terrible life I had lived from the age of four. I was done, over it. I was ready to find joy, and happiness for all of us. *" But the fruit of the Spirit is love, joy, peace, forbearance, kindness, goodness, faithfulness, gentleness, and self-control. Against such things there is no law" Galatians 5:22-23 NIV.* I needed rescued by God not Cameron, but little did I know. I was in love, surely this was what love was. I missed him every day, we talked often, and he kept us all informed of any updates. It was getting closer and closer to being together again.

A month had passed, and Cameron still did not have a place yet. Things were more expensive in Florida than in Missouri. He missed me so much and I missed him. We could not stand to be apart any longer. So, Cameron had asked his family if we could all stay there until one of them got a home for us. Cameron gave us the word; it was time for us to leave. We had a couple of days to get our belongings together, pack the car, and start driving.

Ironically as it sounds, people come into our lives for a reason or a season. For many years, I did not see it that way. I always focused more on the trials, the pain and the hurt people caused in my life rather than the positive things that came out of those situations. Of course, it is not ideal for a young girl to move across state with a boy. Even though, I was too young to be with a guy who was nineteen years old. After we moved to Florida, we never saw Wayne again. *"O LORD, you have searched me {thoroughly} and have known me. You know when I sit down and when I rise up {my entire life, everything I do} You understand my thought from afar. You scrutinize my path and my lying down, And you are intimately acquainted with my ways. Even before there is no word on my tongue {still unspoken} Behold, O LORD, You know it all. Psalm 139:1-4 AMP.*

There was a possibility I did see Wayne one more time, but I do not know for sure. I was working at a fast-food restaurant at the time, working drive-through. I was not sure if it was him, his face had blurred from my memories. As he went through the drive-thru, anxiety twisted in my stomach, sensing something was wrong. An instinct that it was him. There are times when someone has reminded me of him, or certain words that trigger a memory. Those memories can torment me if I allow it. I must get into the word of God, Rinse, and repeat.

I got more excited about what our new life was about to become and to finally be free, to finally feel safe, and not have to continuously look over my shoulder. It took us a couple of days to get to Florida. Once, we saw the Palm trees we knew we were there. The excitement ran through my bones. It was like I had a sugar high. I was bouncing around just waiting and waiting for that moment. The moment I saw Cameron.

We would arrive early in the morning; everyone would still be sleeping. Once we arrived in North Miami, I was supposed to call Cameron. We met up at the nearest gas station in town. We had no idea where we would be staying or what his family was like. We just took a leap of faith that everything would be all right. We trusted Cameron and at that moment that was enough. *"In spite of this you did not trust in the Lord your God." Deuteronomy 1:32 NIV.*

When we make decisions on our own without God, we can cause destruction. We should never put trust in someone above God. Nor should we worship anything other than God. Read the word to recognize the signs of when you are being deceived. When we trust God with our lives and our hearts desires, he will direct us in the right direction. Sometimes when things fall apart, we often find ways it went wrong. Instead of focusing on what God has done for his greater purpose. Everything in life is possible, through God. If you are experiencing difficulty and are unsure of the correct answers. Pray about it, and ask God for guidance. Keep praying and wait upon the Lord.

Prayer-

Dear Heavenly Father,

Thank you for what you have done in my life. Thank you for protecting me when I needed it most. Forgive me for not following your path, and seeking your guidance in my life. I pray that you continue to work on my heart, and my ways so that I can be more like you. In Jesus name I pray. Amen

Once we arrived, I called Cameron, and he met us at the gas station. We arrived in North Miami around 3 am or so. Cameron had us follow him to the beach, we were going to wait there until around 6 am so his family could rest. He would then introduce us to everyone and let us get settled in. The beach was so beautiful, the blue, clear water surrounded with light beige colored sand. I was so excited about this new journey in our life. All I could think about was how free I felt in that moment.

Cameron took me down closer to the water and we walked along the shore. I felt the wet sand in my toes, the cool breeze that chilled my skin, the wind that brushed through my hair, watching the sunset. It was the most beautiful scenery. Everything at that moment just felt right. I can still feel what I felt at that moment, it all seemed as if I was living another person's life. A romantic walk on the beach, like a romantic movie, playing out each scene. It was an amazing feeling, just to feel free. *"The Lord watches over you-the LORD is your shade at your right hand; the sun will not harm you by day, nor the moon by night. The LORD will keep you from all harm-he will watch over your life." Psalm 121:5-7 NIV.* We were a million miles away, Wayne could never hurt us again. Life was going to change; I just knew it.

At that moment in my life, it felt right. However, what we feel is right does not necessarily mean that it is right. If we are not aligned with God's will or what God has planned for us. Our hearts can deceive us, and our emotions can betray us, if we allow it. We all make choices, and those choices have consequences, good or bad. I was too young to make that kind of decision. *"I have the right to do anything, "you say-but not everything is beneficial. "I have the right to do anything"-but not everything is constructive." 1 Corinthians 10:23 NIV.*

I had the right to make the decision, but was it aligned with God's will for my life? I did not have God in my heart, not alone think about what God thought about the plan. I was safe and at that moment I thought it was all I needed. *"God is our refuse and strength, and ever-present help in trouble. Therefore, we will not fear, though the earth give away and the mountains fall into the heart of the sea." Psalm 46:1-3 NIV.* Earlier, I stated God brings people in our lives for a reason or a season. Cameron was in my life for a season. I believe that God takes our bad decisions and turns it too good for his glory. Just wait, my friends. I have just begun to tell my story. It is amazing how I survived. By the grace of God, my Lord and savior, I am breathing today.

We should not worship our circumstances. We should be worshiping God. Looking back on my life at that moment I was worshipping our circumstances and Cameron. I did not have the guidance from my mother to help me make the right decision, but I was old enough to seek God. Pray to God, for his guidance, for the right decision. I still cannot explain as to why those things happened to me; it is not for my own understanding. *Give me understanding {a teachable heart and the ability to learn} that I may keep Your law; And observe it with all my heart"* Psalm 119:34 AMP. I can only hope that my story will speak out to someone else so they too can be healed by the Grace of God.

A few days later, after we arrived in North Miami. We went to the beach again; we loved the beach. It was so beautiful, the light blue sky that glared over the blue-green water. We left all our belongings in our car, clothes, shoes, makeup, everything we owned, our whole life. It was a white four door car. It was a bit rough looking, but it got us where we needed to go. You had to use a screwdriver to start it. It was a car that you could easily steal, and well it was stolen.

When Cameron got home from work, he noticed the car was gone. He asked my mother where her car was. She threw herself in a panic and ran outside and yes it was in fact gone. At first, she had thought Cameron was playing a trick on her. After they had debated for a few minutes, she could tell Cameron was telling the truth. It was not him; the car was stolen. My mother called the police and filed a police report. The police never found the car. *"Why do you stand far away, O LORD? Why do you hide {Yourself, veiling Your eyes} in times of trouble."* Psalm 10:1 AMP. When things happen in life, we tend to thrive off the situation at hand. Instead of, seeking God for guidance. We tend to automatically go into panic mode, and we become angry or frustrated. In these moments, we really need to seek God for guidance to help guide us through tribulations with a more positive attitude.

Cameron was going to help my mother get a job. He set up an interview for her with the landscaping company he worked for. The position was for planting flowers. I can still remember the day my mother went for her interview. She had no idea that they would want her to start that day. She was always taught to dress nicely for an interview no matter what the position is for. "Dress for success, or "Dress for the part." Dress for the part was more like it for that job.

It was a sizzling summer day. My mother was so desperate for a job; she needed the money. We no longer had a car. She had to walk to and from the interview and ended up having to start that day. She was wearing a silky blue dress, panty hose and heels. I can remember her walking down the street later that day with sweat rolling down her face, and her hair was a mess. She looked so exhausted. After that day, she never went back. She was on a mission to find a job more suitable for her. *"I have told you these things, so that in me you may have peace. In this world you will have trouble. But take heart! I have overcome the world." John 16:33 NIV.*

A few days later my mother got a job working at a convenient store working in the deli. She really liked that job. As time went on, we got a place of our own. Cameron had his own place, and we saw each other as often as we could. My sister and I went to school every day until we started to feel unsafe. A few of the kids that went to school carried guns. We never told our mother, we just skipped school. My mother had no idea we were skipping school until the school called. She was ferries with us.

Prayer-

Dear Heavenly Father,

Thank you for providing my mother with a job, thank you for providing us with a home. Father, please forgive me that I didn't see that you were there in those moments, Thank you for protecting me, and providing everything I needed. I am sorry that I didn't thank you enough in those times. In Jesus name I pray. Amen

Our mother was working a lot to provide a home, food, and the things we needed, and we started to run wild. We started back talking to our mother, sneaking out of the house, skipping school, and drinking. We were out of control. *"Start children off on the way they should go, and even when they are old, they will not turn from it." Proverbs 22:6 NIV.* My room had a small window, big enough to crawl out of; it opened like a door. Therefore, we cut the screen out and that was our way out. We would stuff our beds with pillows so our mother would think we were in bed, sneak out the window and head to our boyfriend's house.

In Florida, there was this convenient store that we could walk to and buy alcohol. We would always buy MD 20/20. My sister always got grape flavor, and I got cherry flavor. I was thirteen years old, and my sister was fifteen. They never asked for identification, and people always thought we were Mexican. We had light black to chestnut brown hair, brown eyes, and dark skin. We lived a life that no child should have been able to live. We took advantage of our mother; we were the adults in our eyes. *"Discipline your children, and they will give you peace; they will bring you in the delights your desire." Proverbs 29:17 NIV.*

We needed love from our parents, guidance, structure, love, the need to feel safe, and protected. Our mother failed to give us that and because of it we ran wild, trying to find love in all the wrong places. *"He who withholds the rod {of discipline} hates his son, But he who loves him disciplines and trains him diligently and appropriately {with wisdom and love} Proverbs 13:24 AMP.* We created more chaos and disaster in our life than we needed to. We pushed her so far that she had gotten to the point she had given up trying to get us back in line. *"Let us not grow weary or become discouraged in doing good, for at the proper time we will reap, if we do not give in." Galatians 6:9 AMP.*

My sister got a job working as a server and saved her money to get a place of her own. She was determined not to live under the same roof as our mother. She was done; fed up. I wanted to be just like my sister, so I followed her everywhere she went, her every move. She was my role model; my sister and I faced the world together. I started to skip school to hang out at Cameron's place when he was working. Cameron was my safe place. He really did do everything he could to protect me.

My mother had no idea that I was sexually active with Cameron. I guess she did not realize the impact that Wayne really had on us. She was trying to do her best and we were just walking all over her. I asked her if I could be put on the pill, I did not tell her why. She should have known, why, right? She refused, she said I was too young. She was right, I was too young to have sex. I thought it was normal, no matter what age. I already knew about sex because of what happened to me. She should have let me; it would have been better to be safe.

My sister and I could not find forgiveness in our hearts to forgive our mother. Instead, we did what we wanted, and she had no say about it. *"And whenever you stand praying, if you have anything against anyone, forgive them, so that your Father may forgive you your sins" Mark 11:25 NIV.* My mother did not deserve that treatment from us. Of course, at that time she never asked us to forgive her for the situation she had put us in previously or ever wondered how that all affected us. We could never speak about it, ever. We did not see how hard she really was trying to make things right. We just did not care.

Earlier, I talked about forgiveness. "Why should I forgive; they did not ask for forgiveness? or God does not expect you to forgive if they did not ask for forgiveness. *"If we confess our sins, he is faithful and just to forgive us our sins and purify us from all unrighteousness." 1 John 1:9 NIV.* Holding on to that bitterness, that hatred towards our mother, did nothing but create more chaos. My sister saved her money and got her own place. It was still connected to our mother's apartment. It was an apartment that was right off the side. Like an extra bedroom that had its own access in and out. Can you imagine someone renting an apartment out to a fifteen-year-old girl? She did not have to pay a deposit. All she had to do was pay rent and clean it.

The apartment was so nasty, there were things in there that were offensive, things that was inpatriate. The windows and the door lock were broken. My sister and I fixed it up and then she asked me to move in with her when it was all done. I did not want to leave my mom, but my sister and I were inseparable. I looked up to my sister back then. I was so excited to be roommates with her. It was like we still lived with our mother, it just had more privacy.

My mother did not have the willpower to stop us, we held onto that hatred, resentment, disrespect, and unforgiveness towards her. *"The Lord our God is merciful and forgiving, even though we have rebelled against him"* Daniel 9:9 NIV. How would we ever be able to forgive her, she allowed her boyfriend to touch us, have his way with us. She was in the same room when it happened and never once tried to stop it. We never stopped to think about how she was feeling or what she was going through.

I have always had a relationship with my mother, but I did not always have respect for her because of that trauma. I blamed her for everything, every mistake I made, every unhealthy relationship I engaged in, my insecurities, everything I felt. I would not have been that way if none of that had happened. It should not have happened, but it did. When I became an adult, it was up to me how my life went, not my mothers. I had a choice to break the cycle in my life and make better choices.

When life gives you lemons, make lemonade! I am sure you have heard that quote before, it is an old quote. It means when you go through storms in life, you must make the best of any situation. Sometimes that is hard to do, when you feel as if nothing is going the way you had planned.

I had to get transferred to the new school, by this time you could tell I was pregnant. I was really nervous about going back to school. How were other people going to treat me? I was determined to go back to a regular school. Until the principal told me that I would be treated differently because I was the first girl to come to their school pregnant. They had my classes from upstairs to downstairs, they were everywhere. I was getting closer to having my baby and walking around everywhere was not an innovative idea in my mind.

I told my mother I did not want to go because I was afraid of how people would treat me. The principal said my mother could get in trouble if I did not go. It was the law, and I had to go. I wanted another alternative to get my education without being made as a joke. I understood my situation was not the most ideal for a young girl. I needed my education, but I was determined after the way that principal talked there was no way. I was not going!

I wondered if Brody would be going to the same school. If so, what would people say, what would they do? The next time I saw Brody; he was working at the grocery store. I was still so embarrassed and ashamed of myself. This time you could tell I was pregnant. I could only imagine what he thought about me now. I still could not say anything to him. I just walked right by him as if he was a stranger. I could not explain myself and I did not know how.

My mother called social services to find out my other options. They had stated that the school could not do anything. I was about to have a baby, so I was considered a legal adult. There were certain things I was not allowed to do but I was allowed to make my own choices now. They told her about a program that

Chapter 4

We lived in Florida for less than a year, and things were falling apart. Mom lost her job, we were out of control, skipping school, and drinking. Now my sister was more of a wild one but like I said I wanted to be just like her. Mom had no money to pay the bills or buy food. We had this grapefruit tree in the back yard. I remember that we ate off that tree for a few months breakfast, lunch, and dinner. My sister was working but she had so much resentment towards our mother, she refused to help in any way.

My mother could not find another job, things were getting harder and harder. Cameron had suggested we all moved in together to save money. My mother had agreed with Cameron, so we moved in with him. I thought that it was rad, I got to live with my boyfriend at the age of thirteen. I wanted to take care of him, I wanted to do everything I could to make him happy. Little did I know that he was still infatuated with my sister.

Our relationship started to shift. He finally had the opportunity to have an affair with my sister. One night, we were playing quarters, which is a drinking game. They both had a plot against me, to get me drunk so I would pass out. Then they could have time alone. It did not happen as they had planned. I kept up with them, it was the night my son was conceived. I was a couple of months away from being fourteen years old.

Cameron ended up losing his job, and my mother still had not found a new job. Therefore, they had decided it was time to go back to Missouri. Life was just too hard living in Florida. They had a beautiful beach, and it was a lovely place to visit but no one could get ahead. The cost of living was just too expensive. We packed up our belongings again and prepared to move back to Missouri. Once again, all we took was what we could fit in the car. We left everything else behind.

Cameron had an old Camero, I do not remember the year. We got as far as Georgia when his car broke down and left us stranded. We had no way back to Missouri or anywhere at this have to face Brody because I did not know what to say. I looked so rough and smelled so bad from not having a shower in a few days. I made an unwise decision and there was no coming back from that.

I have thought about that day for thirty-six years. If only, I would have said something, anything to him. I did not even have to say anything about what was going on. I have regretted it my whole life. If only I had made another choice. If only I had said something to Brody that day. An apology would have been an ideal conversation. I have always wondered if my life would be different if I had never broken it off with Brody. If we had never moved to Florida. Now I will never know. I made the choice I did, and there was no going back.

I have lived with so much regret over the course of my life. The wrong decisions, manipulating it in my mind, IF ONLY. *"Do not remember the former things, Or ponder the things of the past. "Listen carefully, I am about to do a new thing, Now it will spring forth; Will you not be aware of it? I will even put a road in the wilderness, Rivers in the desert. Isaiah 43:18-19 AMP.* My life was not aligned with God's will for my life and because of that, I continued to make the wrong decisions. If we seek God's directions, he will direct us on the right path.

We cannot change our past, only our future. As long as I held on to that regret, my life was never going to change. *"In him we have redemption through his blood, the forgiveness of sins, in accordance with the riches of God's grace. Ephesians 1:7 NIV.* I needed to trust that God would work it out for my own good.

Once we got to the motel, we checked in and got situated in our room. Then we walked down to this little grocery store to pick up some groceries. It was within walking distance, so we did not have to walk far. We were so hungry, tired, and needed a shower. My mother had picked up some lunch meat, bread, chips, and something for us to drink. We could not even change into clean clothes, after we took a shower. Our lives were in shackles. We did have each other, and we were safe. We missed what was most important at that moment.

I tried calling Cameron again from the motel and left another message. I wanted to let him know where I was, that I was safe. It appeared that he did not care because at this point, I had tried calling a few times and not once did he ever try to contact me or find me. The first couple of times, I tried to call from a pay phone, telling him where we were. I refused to believe that he did not care. He loved me, I was sure of it. There had to be a reason that he was not looking for me. It was how he broke it off with me without even saying a word. Then again, I refused to believe that was what was going on at that moment.

The next morning, we all walked to the welfare office. My mother was going to try to get more assistance and hopefully they could find us a home. That was her main goal. We got to the welfare office, and they gave us another voucher for a few more days at the motel and two more vouchers for food and clothing. They were also going to help us find a home. I am not even sure what my mother told them the reason we were in that situation. She had no car to go look for work, and she had two teenage daughters to raise. *"So do not worry, saying, "What shall we eat?' or 'What shall we drink?' or What shall we wear?' For the pagans run after all these things, and your heavenly Father knows that you need them. But seek first his kingdom and his righteousness, and all these things will be given to you as well. Therefore, do not worry about tomorrow, for tomorrow will worry about itself. Each day has enough trouble of its own." Matthew 6:31-34 NIV.*

God is amazing isn't he, this verse is so powerful. I feel a chill going straight through me as I am typing the words. Feeling that spirit rushing through me like a cool breeze going straight through my body. As I write my story and apply bible verses to certain situations. I can see how God really was there; he sent help and every time he pulled us out of those situations. It may not have been the way we think it should be. Look back on something in your life , think about it for a minute. It is all in how we decide we want to perceive it. Believe it and you will receive it.

Unfortunately, we all have free will, so it is up to us how we apply these in our lives. God does send us help, even when you cannot see it. He may send people, it may be words from a scripture, a book, a tv show, a sermon, or through a song. It could also be from overhearing someone else's conversation. God will give you the answers you need. You must be paying close attention, or you may miss it. We should also listen to what God is telling us and not take it for our own gain.

After everything we went through, the decision we made, the life we lived, the people we chose. God still found us a way out of each situation. I spent so much of my life thinking about all the terrible things that happened rather than focusing on all the good. All the things, God was doing, and we all took it for granted. We just keep doing what we had thirst for. I honestly did not even notice it until I started writing. I am in awe. I can see how much of a fighter I was. That little faith as a child, god was there saving me each time. God is who gave me that strength to keep pushing through. *"No temptation has overtaken you except what is common to mankind. And God is faithful; he will not let you be tempted beyond what you can bear. But when you are tempted, he will also provide a way out so you can endure it." 1 Corinthians 10:13 NIV.*

The welfare office called, and they had found us a place to live in a town called Archie, Missouri. It was a two bedroom, and we would be moving in three days. We had no furniture, hardly any clothes, money, or food. Mom would always say we had each other and that was all that mattered. She was right, we were together. Even though we had storms after the storms, we were safe.

A few weeks had passed, and I was getting sick every day. I still had not heard from Cameron; it was like he had just vanished. Everything I smelled, I was sick all the time. I was throwing up; it was like I had this bad flu that just would not go away. Mom still did not have a car, but she had made friends with this lady downstairs. Mom said if I did not get any better in the next two days, she would find us a ride to the hospital.

I kept trying to reach Cameron, and one day I finally reached him. He finally came to see me. He came twice and that was the end of that. I do not know why or how I forgave him for leaving me out there like that, but I did. Just because you forgive someone, it does not mean they have to be a part of your life. Just remember that because forgiveness is so powerful through Christ. Allowing someone back into your life and in your heart after hurting you, is another. You can still forgive them and love them from a distance. Do not let the enemy tell you otherwise. He knows how to play tricks on your mind.

One day, I walked into my bedroom that I shared with my sister and saw her writing a letter to Cameron's niece. I was wondering why she was writing her a letter. I tried to be nosy and asked my sister, but she refused to tell me. I tried to grab the letter, but she refused. So, I waited until she was done and then I would find it and read it. She had written about her being in love with Cameron. Oh, how my heart was crushed, my sister, my fleshing blood. How could she? She knew I loved him, but she did not care.

My mother finally took me to the hospital. It had been about four weeks, and I was still getting sick. I had left a note on the door for Cameron in case he showed up and I was gone. I tried to call him but again no answer. The note on the door was telling him that I had been sick, that I was scared, and I needed him to meet me there. When we finally got there, we were waiting for me to be checked in. The hospital was so busy that we waited for a few hours before I got called. There were some tests the doctors wanted to run, and one was a pregnancy test. When we were waiting in the waiting room for the test results, Cameron walked into the hospital with another woman. I glanced over and saw this man, wearing a shirt just like Cameron. When he turned around, I just knew. It was him.

I was crying and terribly upset, Cameron was with someone else. *"But I say to you, love you enemies and pray for those who persecute you," Matthew 5:44 NIV.* He did not even tell me, no explanation, no nothing. When he saw me, they both walked out the door. I went after him, crying and screaming at him. "How could you do this to me? He just kept going, got in his truck, and drove off. My mother was behind me coming after me. Cameron said nothing, completely ignored me. He was such a coward at that moment. I can still feel that ache in my chest of how I felt at that moment.

Mom walked me back into the hospital. It was not much longer when the doctors called me back. The words were finally said, I was pregnant. I was so emotional after I saw Cameron with another woman. The doctors were so concerned about how I reacted to the news. They wanted to put me in a mental hospital. I was barely fourteen years old, and I was pregnant. It was clear I would be on my own. What did they expect me to do, jump up for joy. I was a child, about to have a baby.

The doctors tried to talk my mother in to pressing charges against Cameron for statutory rape because I was a minor. It was wrong to make those accusations against someone. It was not true. *"A false witness will not go unpunished, and whoever pours out lies will not go free." Proverbs 19:9 NIV.* Even though I was too young, I knew what I was doing. I was in an intimate relationship with Cameron. I told my mother NO; she could not do that. He did nothing wrong. Except, cheating on me and moving on with someone else without a word.

I felt like I needed to tell Cameron; he was going to be a father. He had the right to know regardless of what he had done. I had so many decisions to make and I needed him. My mother did not want me to call but I needed to. When I tried to call him, he answered the phone. That was the first time I had ever been able to reach him that fast after we returned from Florida. My mother was on the other line listening to the conversation. When I told Cameron, he said to me, "Well it probably is not mine anyway."

At that moment the thought went through my mind, he has to be joking, seriously. He knew my story and he knew he was my first, except for what men that sexually assaulted me. All my mother said was, we do not need you anyways and hung up. *"Peace, I leave with you; My {perfect} peace I give to you; not as the world gives do I give to you. Do not let your heart be troubled, nor let it be afraid. {Let My perfect peace calms you in every circumstance and give you courage and strength for every challenge.}" John 14:27 AMP.*

That was the last time I heard from Cameron for four years. I had an agonizing decision to make on my own. I was always taught, if you play, you pay. I had that thought replaying in my mind over and over again. I was too young to have a child at my age. I had dreams of having a better life than what my mother provided for me. That I was certain of. Do not get me wrong, I love my mother. However, I wanted a better life for myself, and my children. I wanted to go to college, have a good career, then maybe I would start a family. *"Jesus looked at them and said, "With man this is impossible, but with God all things are possible." Matthew 19:26 NIV.*

Several different people talked to me about my options. There were three options, adoption, abortion, or keeping the baby. I did not believe in abortion so that was excluded. Other people suggested that I should adopt my baby to my mother. If I did, I would still be near, then I would be able to finish school. All I knew was this child deserved a good life. *"Behold, children are a heritage and gift from the Lord, The fruit of the womb a reward." Psalm 127:3 (AMP).*

My decision was not going to be easy. How would I raise a child? I was too young to work, to provide anything for this child. *"Trust in and rely confidently on the Lord with all your heart, and do not rely on your own insight or understanding. In all your ways know and acknowledge and recognize Him, And He will make your paths straight and smooth {removing obstacles that block your way} Proverbs 3:5-6 AMP.*

Do not lean on your own understanding. Those are some powerful words. When we have trials in our lives we need to seek God for direction. Without God we can make bad decisions or get involved in toxic relationships, then we question ourselves. How could I have been so foolish? What did I do to deserve this? How could I have let this happen? How could he or she hurt me this way? When we try and control our lives, we create more chaos and disaster. I will never understand as to why some of things happened in my life. It makes it hard to understand but it is not for my own understanding.

I had no idea what decision to make. I needed God to help direct my path. All I knew was raising a child would be hard when I was so young. I needed to grow up and achieve success to provide for anyone. I had no idea how to raise a child. *" I will instruct you and teach you in a way you should go; I will council you with my loving eye on you. Psalm 32:8 NIV*. I absolutely believe that God takes our story to glorify him. Of course, at the time, I did not see or feel that way. I had all this weight on my shoulders and did not know which way to turn. I was blind, lost, confused, hurt, shameful, and embarrassed of who I was. How would I ever find any glory, with whatever decision I made?

Today, I would rather lean on God to direct my path, than my own. Every decision I have ever made without God has turned into chaos. Throughout my life I continued to see the negative instead of the positive impact it had on my life. For every wrong decision I have made, God turned it into something good. I refused to see everything he was doing in my life.

Prayer-

Dear Heavenly Father,

Thank you, Lord, for loving me, even when I don't seek you as much as I should, thank you for always being by my side and never

leaving me. Thank you for all you have done in my life. In Jesus name I pray.
Amen

God is the only way, he is truth, he is love, the one who can direct you towards the light to see glory. God is who holds the answers, we just have to seek him. No, we may not always get the answers as quickly as we want it but believe me, he answers prayers. *"This is what the Lord, your Redeemer, the Holy One of Israel says, "I am the Lord your God, who teaches you to profit (benefit), Who leads you in the way that you should go." Isaiah 48:17 NIV.*

Chapter 5

Life was getting better again; we were finally stable. Mom had friends that lived downstairs. She still did not have a car, so we were limited to places we could go. We had to walk, or mom would ask her friend to give us a ride. My sister got a job as a server, and well I was still pregnant. Our lives were about to change in a big way. We were very blessed to have this child become a part of our family.

We had a small family, there were no questions about that. My mother had family that lived in Iowa. I do not remember her every reaching out to them very often. We were finally happy again for the most part. My mother's friend had introduced her to someone that was in jail. Well, they ended up becoming pen pals for a while. Mom was meeting people and was finding a way out of this horrific mess our lives had been for the past several years.

We were extremely poor; we did not have very much money. Mom received assistance to help with food and other certain things we needed. " *This poor man cried, and the Lord heard him; he saved him out of all his troubles. Psalm 34:6 AMP.* The food stamps back then were food coupons. It looked like it was fake money, you could only buy food with them. They came in coupon books with tens, five, and one-dollar bills. The food coupons had different presidents on each value coupon. The green ones were ten dollars, purple was worth five dollars, and the copper-colored coupons were one dollar. My mother would give us some dollar food stamps to buy candy to get the change, so she could save the change for cigarettes.

We should not disgrace those who are poor. When we have things to offer, we too should bless those who are facing those same struggles. *"Do to others as you would have them do to you. " Luke 6:31 NIV.* It is God who shows you love, it is God who provides for you, even when we do not deserve it. Bless others, so they too can experience the power of our Lord and Savior. *"And do not forget to do good and to share with others, for with such sacrifices God is pleased. Hebrews 13:16 NIV.* God works in mysterious ways, and even when we cannot see it. He is working for our good. We all make mistakes, we are human. God can show you the way to the light, a brighter future. Believe it and you will receive it.

Sometimes, we take so many things for granted. *"Everything in the world is about to be wrapped up, so take nothing for granted. Stay wide-awake in prayer. Most of all, love each other as if your life depended on it. Love makes up for practically anything. Be quick to give a meal to the hungry, a bed to the homeless— cheerfully. Be generous with the different things God gave you, passing them around so all get in on it: if words, let it be God's words; if help, let it be God's hearty help. That way, God's bright presence will be evident in everything through Jesus, and he'll get all the credit as the One mighty in everything—encores to the end of time. Oh, yes! 1 Peter 4:7-11 MSG.*

It was a hard decision to make about the pregnancy, but I had decided to keep the baby. This child was a part of me, and I could not bear the thought of never seeing him again. I was going to have a little boy. I was scared to become a mother at such an immature age. I had no clue what I was doing, it just felt right. My mother allowed me to make my own choice. She said she would stand by me no matter what I decided. A child that I could love, a child that could love me. This child was a blessing in my life, even when I did not see it at that moment.

I was seven months pregnant when I met someone new. He was a relative of my mother's friends. He was from California, visiting his family. He had been in a motorcycle accident and had a cast on his left leg from a motorcycle accident. He had between dish-water blonde hair and noticeably light brown hair, and deep brown eyes. He was nineteen years old, handsome, skinny, a shorter kind of guy; but extremely attractive. He was so attractive that even my sister liked him. Oh boy, here we go again!

His name was Damon, he was a nice guy. Nicer than anyone I had ever met before. His was very polite, a gentleman. We visited my mother's friends, and Damon was there. The first night I met him, he asked me to dance to a song that was playing on the radio. We were in his brother's living room just visiting when he randomly asked me to dance. I do not remember what song it was. Yes, it was hard for us to dance but we did! He had a cast on his leg, and I was seven months pregnant. I had a big round, fat belly, so there was a big space between us.

Damon did not live in Missouri and was only there for an abbreviated time. He was heading back to California in a week. I never thought I would ever see him again. He was such a nice person. I was a young girl who was about to have a baby. Even so, he was so kind to me. It seemed as if it did not even bother him. Not as much as I made myself feel. How would I ever find love? Could anyone love me? I had this horrific past that all I could see was the ugly. It really did not matter if he liked me or not? I was too young to have a child, to be in another relationship. He was leaving anyway. There was no sense in wrapping my head all around what could be.

When we feel negatively, and doubt ourselves, we put out a negative vibe to others. *"But when you ask, you must believe and not doubt, because the one who doubts is like a wave of the sea, blown and tossed by the wind. James 1:6 NIV.* This way of thinking is very unhealthy for our bodies as well as others around us. We make decisions we wish we could change; we are human. We need to stop tormenting ourselves about what was and focus on what is, at this moment. Have confidence in ourselves and believe in what the Lord says. Remember, God created us in his image. So, if God created us, does that mean God made a mistake? God loves us and wants the best for us. We have to retrain our minds in the image of God, and we will build more confidence about who God created us to be.

Eventually, we ended up moving back to Harrisonville, Missouri. We found this apartment called Thunderbird Apartments. My mother's friend moved there as well and got an apartment right underneath us. It was a nice apartment. We were all doing great.

was called home schooling. There would be a teacher that would come out once a week that would help me do my studies. I could still graduate with a diploma.

Somehow over time Wayne found us again. I have no idea how, but he did. He went to my mother's friend's apartment that lived right below us. Her friend had the same name. That is how there was a mix up, I guess. My mother's friend had no idea who he was. We never told anyone about Wayne, it was our secret. Somehow, he had found out I was pregnant. Wayne had told me if I had ever gotten pregnant, he would kill me. I have never forgotten those words. I never saw him, only my mother. She took control and stopped him from getting to me. God was protecting me and my child. *"He hushed the storm to a gentle whisper, so that the waves of the sea were still." Psalm 107:29.*

God gave my mother strength to stand strong. When we live in a negative environment and have negative attitudes, negative things happen. When we live in a positive environment and have positive attitudes, positive things happen. The thoughts that struggle through our minds are a battlefield. For so many years, I focused so much on the negative things that continued to happen in my life. Writing this book has opened my eyes to more possibilities, if only I believe. All the things that God was doing in my life, which passed me right on by without a blink.

This is still only the beginning of my story. All those years of fighting through depression, God was there. How do I know this? Because, each situation I went through, God found a way to pull me out of it. The moment I started to think about the positive things that came out of it. The happier I was, the more I wanted to help people who faced challenging times. *"The LORD is my shepherd, I lack nothing. He makes me lie down in green pastures, he leads me beside quiet waters, he refreshes my soul. He guides me along the right paths for his name's sake." Psalm 23:1-3 NIV.*

In January nineteen ninety, my son was born. I say it is my son because his father has not been in his life very much over the years. Allen weighed six pounds, five ounces and was twenty-one inches long. He was bold headed, noticeably light skin and was as cute as a button. The first time, I held him in my arms, it was love at first sight. He was so tiny, and small. It was up to me to protect him, guide him, love him, comfort him, and teach him. I had to become this mother, that I had no clue of how to be. I just knew in that moment, I would somehow.

I was still doing the home schooling and trying to do my studies. I was so determined to give this child a better life somehow. I was still too young to work, to make money and support my child. My mother was able to get more assistance to help with the care of my son. I received WIC to help with the formula. I did not breastfeed, I thought it was weird, so I fed him with a bottle. I was nowhere financially capable of caring for this little person. One thing I knew for sure was no-one could love him like me.

A few months after my son was born, Damon had decided to move back to Missouri. He wanted to be closer to his family. He was kind, gentle, loving, and handsome. We began to spend more time together and I fell in love with him. Every time he touched me, I felt this strong connection, this love I never thought was possible. He was the one person that I knew genuinely loved me.

We were too young to start a family together. I do not regret him ever becoming a part of my life. I am not even sure if we genuinely loved each other. Maybe, I just felt he was my safe place. I do not believe it was true love, because if it was, we should have made it through the challenging times. *"Beyond all these things put on and wrap yourselves in {unselfish} love, which is the perfect bond of unity {for everything is bound together in agreement when each one seeks the best for others}." Colossians 3:14 AMP.* I had no clue of what a normal relationship looked like. His parents had a healthy relationship. They stayed married for several years, until the day they left this world. They were the first couple in my existence at the time that was normal.

I had all these baggage's that needed to be dealt with. I could not love anyone all those years ago. I did not even love myself. I still held onto that shame, the guilt, all that baggage. *"Let us lie down in our shame, and let our dishonor and humiliation cover us; for we have sinned against the Lord our God, we and our fathers; from our youth even to this day we have not obeyed the voice of the Lord our God." Jeremiah 3:25 AMP.* I could not seem to let go of the things that had happened to me. All I wanted was to be loved and to feel safe. Was I even worthy of being loved?

When we recognize that things in our life are toxic. We hold on to all the shame, guilt, unworthiness, unhappiness, bitterness, hatred, and try to take things in our own control. Our spirit is dying! *"Hatred stirs up conflict, but love covers over all wrongs." Proverbs 10:12 NIV.* If we ask God for forgiveness, repent our sins, cleanse our body from all the uncleanliness. *"See to it that no one fails to obtain the grace of God; that no 'root of bitterness' springs up and causes trouble, and by it many become defiled." Hebrews 12:15 NIV.* We are reborn in Christ. Allow God to cleanse you from all the hurt, shame, guilt, depression, addiction, bitterness, hatred. Whatever it is you need to be cleansed from to live a more positive life in the eyes of Christ.

We should not rely on others to feel loved, safe, or provided for. When we look for all these things in a relationship without God, we end up in the wrong relationships. We should not be ashamed of our journey. *"However, if you suffer as a Christian, do not be ashamed, but praise God that you bear that name." 1 Peter 4:16 NIV.* It took me several years to let go of the regret. I am no longer ashamed of my life journey. There are things I wish I could have done differently, but it is now only my past. I have to continue to look forward, learn how to embrace it, to trust in God, what he has planned for me, and have faith he will send the right people in my life.

Chapter 6

My mother always had financial struggles when I was growing up. We were extremely poor. I know it could not have been easy raising two girls on her own. She had no help from anyone. We ended up in shelters because we had nowhere to go. Now, there were four of us. I added on another mouth to feed, and another person my mother had to worry about. This was not the life I wanted for him, but I was still too young to work.

There were times my mother would park the car at rest areas, it is where we would sleep. Of course, those times where before my son was born. I can only assume she tried to escape Wayne and that is why we had nowhere to go. I never asked her why because it is the past. Everything that I went through is only memories. Looking back on those memories and where I am today. I am in awe. How did I ever get through it all?

Damon and I were still seeing each other quite often. He lived with his parents in the basement of his brother's house. They had it set up just like a studio apartment. It was a cozy little place. There was a brown pull-out couch, and a kitchen table set. Damon had a room that was separated by a curtain. Behind that curtain was a bed where we slept. There was another curtain that separated a place to use the restroom. It had a five-gallon bucket with a toilet lid. We mostly used it in the middle of the night, so we did not have to go upstairs. I know how weird that might sound today but it worked.

When we have trivial things in life, we appreciate the finer things. When we grow up with a horrific past, we intend to dwell on our past. We can no longer control it or change it. If we accept God into our lives and acknowledge him, he can wash us clean from all the uncleanliness that holds into our spirit. *"In all your ways know and acknowledge and recognize Him, and he will make your paths straight and smooth {removing obstacles that block your way}." Proverbs 3:6 AMP.* We have one or two choices: either let those struggles define and destroy us or we can learn from them, and trust in the Lord to direct us on the right path. *"In their hearts humans plan their course, but the LORD establishes their steps." Proverbs 16:9 AMP.*

We can hold on to the hurt, resentment, hatred, anger, frustration, bitterness and create more chaos and disaster. I know I did it for several years. I had so much hate and anger built up inside me that it nearly destroyed me. "Your past does not define you, only your future." We live in a corrupt world, but we all have a choice. Seek God and he will direct our path. *"The Lord directs the steps of the godly. He delights in every detail of their lives. "The LORD makes firm his steps of the one who delights in him; though he may stumble, he will not fall, for the LORD upholds him with his hand." Psalm 37:23-24 AMP.*

Those painful memories are still with me. There are still things that make my heart ache. I am stronger today, but I always have my eyes wide open. I can never change my past, all I can do is keep reaching for the Lord to give me strength to keep pushing through. No one said life was easy. For every breath we take, every moment we have, we should just embrace it. Be thankful for what we have, appreciate the people around us that love us. Tomorrow is never promised.

I was with Damon so much that I got kicked out of the homeless shelter. In the nineties they had what is called a Metro bus. You could take that bus just about anywhere around the city. I would take a bus from the shelter to Damon's all the time. I loved being with him. I hated it when we were apart. He gave me security, hope, and love. Damon and his family made me feel safe. He was the one I wanted to spend the rest of my life with.

My mother finally got us another place to live, and we moved to Independence. I had this big bedroom that was big enough for both my son and me. I dropped out of school and took care of my son. *"Behold, children are a heritage from the Lord, the fruit of the womb a reward. Psalm 127:3 AMP.* I did not feel comfortable with anyone caring for my child. It was my responsibility to protect him, to keep him safe, to care for him, and to love him. I had planned that I would study to get my GED (General Education Diploma). At that moment, I thought I was doing the right thing. *"Train up a child in the way he should go {teaching him to seek God's wisdom and will for his abilities and talents}, Even when he is old, he will not depart from it." Proverbs 22:6 AMP.*

God blessed me with this child, for some reason or another. I still do not understand as to why. The choice I made to raise my son always felt was vile because he deserved better. A better life than my family or I could give him. *"For You formed my innermost parts; You knit me {together} in my mother's womb. I will give thanks and praise to You, for I am fearfully and wonderfully made; Wonderful are Your works, and my soul knows it very well." Psalm 139:13-14 AMP.* I was determined to make a better life for my son. I would go back to school, get a good education, a decent job and someday we would never have to worry about finances or anyone ever hurting us. No one to come in and destroy us.

Prayer-

Dear Heavenly Father,

"Thank you for blessing me with this child to love. Lord, I apologize for not seeing that you were right by my side, just waiting for me to knock at the door. I am sorry, I did not ask for your help when I needed your guidance more than anyone else's. Thank you for loving me and carrying me throughout my journey even when I didn't deserve your love. In Jesus Name I pray.

Amen

When I became a mother, I was fourteen and a half years old. I was determined that I would never let anyone hurt my child. Everything in my life was about him now. He was an innocent child, a gift that God brought into this world. The moment I was able to see that, the less I felt shameful of being a young mother. People will pass judgement on others for their life choices. However, what others say about us is none of our business. I believe what the LORD says about me.

Over the years, I have questioned myself if I made the right choice. If I should have given him up for adoption. All I knew was I could love him unconditionally and at that moment it was enough. I needed guidance from God. He could have been whomever I needed him to be. A mother, a father, a husband, a brother, a sister. I refused to go to church or believe God was doing any good in my life. I knew how I would be disowned, disgraced, and judged if I stepped into any church. I had a child out of wedlock. I could never be forgiven. I was unworthy of God's love. This was all a lie; a lie the enemy told me. The enemy will come to kill, steal, and destroy.

In the world I grew up in; It was a sin to have a child and not be married. It was a sin to have sex prior to marriage. God would not accept me; I was not worthy of his love. I lived my life around what other people thought about me, listening to all those judgements. I carried that shame, guilt, and confusion around with me. I carried those burdens so high on my shoulders that it felt like I was carrying a ton of bricks. I believed this about myself most of my life.

Eventually, I ended up moving in with Damon. My sister moved out and got married at the age of seventeen. Mom moved to a town called Moberly to be closer to her mate. She was still writing letters to that guy that was in jail. I did not want to go; this guy was in jail. I wanted no part of it. I loved Cameron and I was not about to move hundreds of miles away from him. I wanted to stay, and I am so thankful that his parents allowed me too. My sister and I did not want the life our mother was providing anymore. I eventually found my own path of destruction.

Nine months after Allen was born, Damon and I got married. I was fifteen years old when I got married for the first time. My mother showed up one day and said she received a letter from social services. The letter stated that she had abandoned Alex and me. It was not true of course. I fell for it, and I believed her. *The Lord detests lying lips, but he delights in people who are trustworthy." Proverbs 12:22 AMP.* All my mother wanted was for me to come back home with her. Moberly was about two and a half hours away. I did not understand as to why she wanted me to come back home. There was no way I wanted to go through what we had before. I did not want to leave Damon either; I was finally happy.

Damon did not want me to go either. We loved each other so there had to be another way. I was finally safe; he had good parents. They were the kind of parents that worked through things together, loving, and caring. I do not ever remember a time I saw them ever fighting. They were married for several years. They had their battles I am sure, but they worked through them. They accepted me into their home, their family. I am sure they did not agree with a lot about Damon and me. However, they still accepted me.

Thirty years later I found out the truth about the day I got married. My mother had lied about the letter. She did not give me a lot of explanation except that she wanted me to come back home with her. I should have or I was right where I needed to be. She would take her daughters to jail with her to see this man. I did not want to be in a situation again like we were before. *"Do not judge, or you too will be judged. For in the same way you judge others, you will be judged, and with the measure you use, it will be measured to you " Matthew 7:1-2 NIV.* Damon and I loved each other very much. He thought about every conceivable way for me to stay.

Damon and I planned a wedding in two days. We were going to the chapel, and we were getting married. Damon wanted a church wedding, a wedding under God's oath. *"Therefore, what God has joined together, let no one separate." Mark 10:9 NIV.* We got married in a small white church in Greenwood. I do not remember much about what my wedding dress looked like except it was an

Ivory color. I had been told that God would not allow me to wear white. God does not believe in sex before marriage. I had a child out of wedlock; therefore, I was not pure. This was a lie. Had I repented, God would have forgiven me.

So many people in this world refuse to go to church because of the beliefs they grew up on. We believe in the lies of the enemy that we are not worthy of God's love. Remember, no matter what your situation is or what you have done. God loves you and wants us to turn from our ways and seek him. *"Do not let your heart be troubled (afraid, cowardly). Believe {confidently} in God and trust in Him, {have faith, hold on to it, rely on it, keep going and} believe also in Me. In My Father's house are many dwelling places. If it were not so, I would have told you, because I am going there to prepare a place for you." John 14:1-2 AMP.* We need to see the vision of our LORD and Savior in our lives. He will determine our destination; he can also create our destiny. He has a mission for us to speak the word, the truth, and we will have eternal life. *"For God so loved the world that he gave his one and only Son, that whoever believes in him shall not perish but have eternal life." John 3:16 NIV.*

I was so happy that I was about to begin this new journey in my life with Damon. Now it was my time, I had to do this right. I had to be a good mother and a good wife. At that moment, our little family was the most precious thing in my life. Damon accepted my son as if he were his own. The first couple of years our marriage was great. Do not get me wrong, we had our struggles. Eventually, over time we grew apart. We were both so young and went in different directions.

I still fought with a lot of demons inside of me because of my past. It affected a lot of my emotions, and I always felt so alone. Always remember, you are never alone. God is always with you, always there to give you comfort whenever you need it. He is there to hold you when you feel you can barely hold on. Just hold on a little longer, he will not let you fall. *" The LORD is near to the brokenhearted and he saves those who are crushed in spirit (contrite in heart, truly sorry for their sin)." Psalm 34:18 AMP.* I struggled with trust all my life, which eventually caused problems in my relationships. I could not trust anyone, and I barely trusted in God.

Sometimes, when Damon went out with his friends. I could not go because I was too young to go to some of the places they went. I also had a child to take care of. There was one place we got to go together. It was the one place where I could feel like I was part of his world. He would take me to a place in Peculiar, and we would just dance. Do you know that song "You look wonderful tonight," by Eric Clapton? He made me feel like I was the most beautiful lady out there on that dance floor. I felt like that every time we went out dancing!

We should never dictate our lives based on how someone else makes us feel. I spent so much of my life depending on others to make me happy. I had to find happiness, love and accept myself for who I was. We are not perfect. We all have flaws. We have to recognize our weakness and seek God to help change our ways, our thoughts, our decisions. Sometimes we have to stand alone to find joy and happiness in the Lord to shape us to be the person he designed us to be. We can only change our destination through Christ.

Damon and I had eventually moved to Peculiar and lived in a trailer with his parents. They had a wring washer. Do you remember those? So, it is a metal washer that has a square tub, and it is about twenty-three inches deep. At the top of the washer is a ringer that has a handle with two rollers. You had to put the clothes in the tub to wash them, then ring them out. You would turn that handle and feed the clothes through the rollers one by one. After the wash is done, you put the clothes back into the tub with clean water to be rinsed, and ring them out again. Then hang them outside on the line to dry.

His parents lived in a very old-fashioned way. We did not have hot water. We had to boil water for baths and wash dishes. These things taught me life skills. Do not get me wrong, it was dreadful.

However, everything I learned, every struggle, every storm, every obstacle taught me how many things in life we take for granted. I have learned how to stretch on things and make a dollar last. Today, we have so many opportunities that are taken for granted. Times were tougher back then.

We had little resources back in the nineties. You had to earn every dollar you made; stretch every penny you had. We had no babysitters, and we learned most on our own. Now I am grateful there was a woman who came along the way who taught me many things. She taught me how to cook, do laundry, and gave me tips on how to care for my child. She taught me things about being a wife, and things I needed to survive.

Everything in this world, God has provided. When I say everything, I literally mean everything. People, money, cars, food, homes, accessories. We should all be so very thankful for everything he has provided for our use. We cross paths with people that may not always turn out the way we hoped but there are positive things that come out of those situations. We just have to see it, stop looking for everything that went wrong and look for the things that went right.

After I turned sixteen, I got pregnant again. Damon and I were going to have our first child together. I remember the day we found out. We had taken his mother to the hospital to have some test done. While we were there waiting for her to be done, we went to have a pregnancy test done. We were standing in the elevator when we told his mom. We were going to have a baby. We were so excited; we had been planning this pregnancy, and it happened.

The first couple of years of our marriage were fairly good. We ended up moving to California and started a life there. Our daughter was born on September thirteen nineteen ninety-two. She was so beautiful, so precious, so stunning and so innocent. She was born with a full head of black hair, brown eyes, and beige colored skin. She was so dark she looked like a Mexican baby. She took my breath away. I was so excited to have a girl. Pretty dresses, bows, shoes, she was going to have everything I could give her. I was going to do everything in my power to always protect her, both my children.

The day she was born, Damon and I went to see a movie and stopped to see a friend on the way home. After we arrived home, we went directly to bed. I could not sleep that night because it felt like I had to pee. I kept waking up with the urge to go. Our bathroom was not far from our bedroom. Thank goodness because it was like every fifteen minutes I was headed to the bathroom. On the last trip, I started walking back to bed when I felt this gush of water that splashed all over the floor. It was like dumping a bucket of water and let me tell you it was a mess.

I knew at that moment it was time for my precious little girl to be born. I was so excited but scared at the same time. Damon was sound asleep and trying to wake him was impossible. When I finally woke him, he was like "are you sure this time. Yes, I was sure my water broke, there was no question about it now. We finally got to the hospital. It was a long, painful labor. I had complete back labor and let me tell you that was the longest and most painful labor I had ever experienced. She was a blessing in my life, the moment she was born and the moment I held her in my arms. I totally and completely fell in love all over again.

We lived in a town called Modesto, California. Damon was not around much after our daughter was born. We now have two children, I definitely have a family now. Damon started hanging out with his friends more. I stayed home and took care of the kids. I had my hands full, it was overwhelming at times. He was never there to help, he was not there to be a husband or a father. The pressure started to build up, but I never said a word. I did what I was supposed to do, cook, clean, take care of my children, and my husband. *"Consider it pure joy, my brothers, and sisters, whenever you face trials of many kinds, because you know that the testing of your faith produces perseverance. Let perseverance finish its work so that you may be mature and complete, not lacking anything." James 1:2-4 NIV.*

We did not have a car, so getting to places made things harder. I did not know how to drive. I did have a bike, but it was hard to get places with two children on a bike. Damon bought me that bike when I was pregnant. I would ride the bike with my son in the carriage to the laundry mat. I had a shopping bag of dirty clothes on each handlebar, making several trips until I got all the laundry to wash. It was not fun by any means. When our daughter came, there was no way I could ride that bike with a baby and a toddler. Life was definitely a struggle back then.

Even though I had this family, I still felt like something was missing in my life. I thought maybe If I had found my father, I would be complete. We did not have internet, computers, or cell phones in nineteen ninety-two. We had four one-one. You could call that number to find a listing for a certain person. I did not know much about my father; all I knew was what was on my birth certificate. It had been thirteen years since my father left. I called information and asked for a listing of my father's name in the town where I was born. They only had one listing with the letter and the last name. It was only one phone number, but I had to try. *"And we know {with great confidence} that God {who is deeply concerned about us} causes all things to work together {as a plan} for good for those who love God, to those who are called according to His plan and purpose." Romans 8:28 AMP.*

That one phone number was my Aunt. This was totally a God moment. I had prayed for many years my father would find me but instead I found him. I was many steps closer to finding him, with a total of just two phone calls. Of course, my aunt would not give me my father's phone number. She said she would call my grandmother and see what she said about it. They had apparently received many calls with people stating they were my father's child. I gave my aunt all the information that was listed on my birth certificate. I did not have much information, but it was enough.

I waited by the phone hoping and praying this was the moment I had waited for. I was anxiously waiting for the phone to ring.

Now, I was thinking it would be my grandmother that was going to call. However, when the phone rang, I answered. It was my father on the other side of the receiver. When I heard his voice, he said this is your father. I was in tears; I had waited so long for that day. It was a prayer that was finally answered. *"Before they call I will answer, while they are yet speaking I will hear."* Isaiah 65:24 NIV.

I started to build a relationship with my father over the phone. I lived in Modesto, California, and he lived in San Antonio, Texas. Of course, my father was not happy about my life choices. I was married and already had two children at the age of seventeen. Regardless, of what he thought at the time. We still tried to have a relationship. He sent me things for my daughter. He sent several different baby items for her. He had also sent me three hundred dollars to buy a car. I have consistently thought that it was his way of making up for all the years he missed.

My father convinced Damon and I to drive down so we could meet. We had a car now, thanks to my father. It was a hunter green nineteen seventy-four Plymouth Valiant four door car. Damon drove us to San Antonio, Texas to meet my father. To me it was like meeting him for the first time in my life. I was so excited to finally meet him. How would we know who each other was? Somehow, we knew. We met up at a convenience store and once my father got out of his car, I knew immediately he was my father.

On our trip, my father took me shopping in Old Mexico. He told me about my ancestors, where his family originated. He showed me this picture he carried around in his wallet when I was about six years old. Apparently, my mother had sent it to his mother and that is how he got it. He told me I was a quarter Spanish; I am actually more because I took more of my father's genetics. I recently took a DNA that shows I am thirty three percent Spanish. I needed to see if my father was telling me the truth all these years. Our relationship was rocky for the first ten years.

Damon and I stayed in California for about a year and headed back to Missouri. We went to stay with his parents for a while until we got a place of our own. Damon got a job doing landscaping. I could not work because I had two children to take care of and no one to babysit. We couldn't afford childcare. When I tried to get a job, I worked two hours and then quit. Damon had a lot of pressure on him trying to provide for all of us financially. I was overwhelmed with all the mom and wife duties. My husband was hardly ever home. We were both so broken that we didn't know how to healthy argument, to be true to each other, and work through our difference.

There was a time I remember he got really violent was over a poem I had written. He was for sure; I had written it about his cousin. It was not about no one really. My sister was the one who had a crush on his cousin not me. I was married to Damon, and I did not want anyone else. Damon felt so bad for what he did that he called the police on himself. He admitted to the police officers what he had done, and he went to jail. I did not press charges, so he was released the next day.

I was taken off all the time, heading to my mom's place in Moberly. Every time, something was not right I would leave. I was so emotionally broken. Whenever I felt unsafe, hurt, scared, unworthy I would run. There were demons in my spirit that made me believe I was never good enough for anyone. Men were going to treat me bad and that was that. It would be good for a while and then it would all turn to rubbish. Damon had taught me how to drive. Once I learned how to drive, got my license, and got a car I left for good.

Chapter 7

I told Damon that I needed some time to think. I was going to go to my mom's for a while. I was so overwhelmed with raising children and being a wife. I never had the life I should have had. I never really got to be a kid, a teenager. Damon convinced me to leave our daughter with him. I was not about to leave my son because he had no say about that. Our daughter was a little over a year old. I should not have let him talk me into it, but I did. It was his daughter too.

It was just his security keeping our daughter. If he had her, he knew that I would come back. He knew how much I loved our daughter and there was no way that I would leave her. It was going to be a long drive to Moberly. I did not have my license for exceptionally long. It was my first trip driving that far alone. I was getting tired, so I pulled over to a motel to get some rest. Damon had followed me all the way to the motel, or he had figured out where I was. I never asked how he found me.

He had took a spark plug off my car, so that it would not start. When I tried to start it, it blew sparks. It was like it was going to catch fire. *"Do not say, "I'll pay you back for this wrong!" Wait for the LORD, and he will avenge you." Proverbs 20:22 NIV.* There was a gentleman walking around outside that offered to help me. Damon was still somewhere watching. He was so sure that I was having an affair, but I was not. I had no idea who that person was that tried to help me. All I wanted to do was get the car started and start driving.

I called my mother because the car was not going to start. I had no idea what was wrong. Mom's boyfriend was out of jail by this time. So, he brought my mother to get me. Since it was so late, we left my car. We were going to come back and get it the next day. I should have taken everything out of the car that night. My children's Christmas presents were in the trunk. I did not have very much money and that was all I had for them. When we went back to get the car the next day, it was gone.

Damon took the car. He later had it completely crushed. Anyways, that is what I heard. Damon was so angry that I had left, he plotted revenge. He was going to make sure that I did not go anywhere. He threatened me about not letting me have our daughter back. After everything he did, I grew more hatred towards him. He wanted to believe that I was cheating when I was not. Nothing I said was going to matter. All he wanted was for me to come back home.

When we react out of our emotions, we create destruction, chaos, bitterness, and hatred. This is what the enemy wants; he wants you to turn to his ways. *"Indeed, it was for my own well-being that I had such bitterness; But You have loved back my life from the pit of nothingness (destruction), For You have cast all my sins behind Your back." Isaiah 38:17 AMP.* He tries to get into our minds to make us believe things that are not there, or things that are not true. The enemy wants you to believe that God will never love you or forgive you. The enemy will come to kill, steal, and destroy. *"The Lord said to my Lord "Sit at my right hand until I make your enemies a footstool for your feet." Luke 20:42-43 NIV.* God will show you Grace, repent, ask for forgiveness and he will forgive.

God sacrificed his only son by sending him to earth to be crucified on the cross. He did all this for our sins. Why, would he do such a thing you ask? Because God so loved the world that he gave his one and only Son, that whoever believed in him shall not perish but have eternal life. Jesus offers us a chance for salvation and redemption; he encourages sinners to turn away from sin and transform their lives into the image of Christ.

We need to turn our ways, our hearts, our paths, our emotions, our actions, and our feelings towards God. He is the one who will heal our hearts, he will show us forgiveness, give us grace, and forgive us for the things we have done. God will show us all these things, and all we must do is accept it, receive it, and believe it, and we will receive the blessing of God. We must show those same things to others, even after all they have done. Forgive others as God has forgiven us. Love our neighbor as God loves us. *"Love is patient, love is kind. It does not envy, it does not boast, it is not proud. It does not dishonor others, it is self-seeking, it is not easily agreed, it keeps no records of wrongs. Love does not delight in evil but rejoices with the truth. It always protects, always trust, always hopes, always perseveres."* 1 Corinthians 13:4-7 NIV.

We are all human, and it is quite easy to react out of our emotions. I know I did; I still must practice it every day. Reminding myself who God is and what he has done for me. God wants us to turn to his ways and get others to follow. The moment we turn away from God's words, destruction will soon follow. When I do not stay in the word of God, I can see myself falling right back into all the pain in my heart. Believing all those things that are not true. I will believe what the Lord says about me. God has delivered me, and I am a child of God. I am still a work-in-progress.

Damon and I were separated for about three months. I had decided that I wanted to start a life of my own. I wanted to pursue my dreams. I had been trying for two years to get my GED, but I was not successful. Damon was not incredibly supportive of me getting my education. He was not even supportive when I was asked to become a model for a cosmetic company. I was a full-time mother and full-time wife. It felt as if everything was crushing me. I could not breathe. I needed a change. I kept having those thoughts of self-worth that just never seemed to go away.

I was seventeen years old when I got an apartment of my own. I was going in the right direction to get my life on the right path. Damon still had our daughter. It took me a few weeks before I landed my first job. I waited several weeks before someone called me. I had no prior experience; so that did not help. My first job was at a fast-food restaurant. I was going to start working in the kitchen, working on the broiler. The broiler was where they had cooked hamburger patties. Standing behind a broiler for eight hours a day was not my idea of a future.

Damon had finally decided to let me have our daughter back. She was going to come live with me. I was so excited the day she came home with me; we stayed up all night playing and spending time together. I did not care that I had to be at work at five in the morning. I had my daughter and at that moment it was all that mattered. Even though I was a young mother, my children are my world. They mean everything to me. They are the ones that helped me to keep going, to fight harder. I wanted so much to be the best mother I could be.

Along the way, I made several wrong decisions. I was still so lost, confused, and ashamed of myself. I was ashamed of the things that happened to me, ashamed that I was a young mother, ashamed of leaving my husband. I had no idea how to be happy. I held onto all the hurt, shame, and guilt for so long that it destroyed me. Being a young mother was far from being easy. I gave up my teenage life, my education, and my dreams.

Sometimes things do not always work out the way we plan. We cannot seem to look past the life we were dealt with. We need to reach for God, so that we can embrace those experiences in life. *"No one has ever seen God; but if we love one another, God lives in us and his love is made complete in us" 1 John 4:12 NIV.* I continued to live my life in chaos and disaster. It was not fair or right that I had to go through all this, and I was only seventeen. I struggled so hard as a young mother. I never stayed at one job for exceptionally long. Every time someone said or did something I did not like. I would run.

Things in life are only temporary. No matter what journey life has taken you. There is always hope. Believing in God, trusting in God has completely turned my life into something that was so tragic into something beautiful. *"You, Lord are forgiving and good, abounding in love to all who call to you" Psalm 86:5 NIV.* Each breath we are given is a blessing. Each day God gives us another day, to change our ways. A day to decide to believe and to trust in his ways. God's way is the only way. You will find hope, love, kindness, compassion, and forgiveness. All these are found in the word of God. *"Be kind and compassionate to one another, forgiving each other, just as in Christ God forgave you"* Ephesians 4:32 NIV.

Damon and I had tried to work on our marriage a few times. He would come down to Moberly to see us. There were times I went back home with him. It just seemed like I could not let go. I could not forgive him for the things he had done. There were times he reacted out of that hurt, that just created more disaster. I created more chaos out of hatred. We both just kept hurting each other more than we needed to. We needed to let go of each other. Honestly, we needed God to heal us.

I had tried to go back several times; I was just so unhappy. I felt like I was giving up on everything. I was determined that I was going to have a better life for my children and for myself. I did rotten things out of that hurt and cheated on Damon; with a man I do not even remember today. I felt ignored by my husband. When someone showed me attention, my eyes wondered. I took that hurt that Damon caused me and repaid him with revenge. I carried that guilt around with me for over thirty years. *"Let us draw near to God with a sincere heart and with the full assurance that faith brings, having our hearts sprinkled to cleanse us from a guilty conscience and having our bodies washed with pure water."* Hebrews 10:22 NIV."

During our last separation, we conceived another child. There were so many people who believed that it was not his child. I am going to confess; I was dating someone else several weeks prior. I had broken it off because I wanted to make my marriage work. I took off and went back home to be with my husband. He was still partying a lot, running with his friends, there was so much anger that was built around us. All the burdens that I carried and the way he was living his life. I just could not do it anymore.

I left Damon for the last time. I was nineteen years old and pregnant with my third child. I knew it was going to be hard. Regardless, I was determined that I could do it. I needed to find a way to get back to school and get my education. Trying to work full-time and trying to go to school just wasn't working. I was still so overwhelmed that I couldn't breathe. I was directing my path, instead of allowing God to lead me the way. No matter how hard I tried, I just kept failing. *"Have mercy on me, Lord, for I am faint; heal me, Lord, for my bones are in agony." Psalms 6:2 AMP.*

When I was a few months pregnant with my third child. I was driving my sister's car and ended up in a bad car accident. I thought my life was about to end. My mother and my children and two of my nephews were with me. A car was speeding down the road, T-boned us from the driver's side. The car that hit us came out of nowhere and in the blink of an eye, our lives were shattered. My legs were crushed between the driver's door and the seat. My nephew's face got pretty banged up and the other children came out with no scratches. My mother had two punctures in her lungs, and I was in serious condition. The paramedics had to cut the car door to get me out. Three of us were taken to the hospital, it was so terrifying. The car that hit us came out of nowhere. Speeding down the road, and in the blink of an eye, our lives were shattered.

My mother and I were transferred to another hospital. They did not have the proper medical equipment to give us proper care. My mother and I were both transferred by life flight. It was the scariest moment I have ever experienced. We were not sure if we were going to make it. I did not have a seat belt on, which is the law. However, it was what saved my life. I had a fractured hip, and a broken pelvis. There was water leaking around the bag that protects the baby during pregnancy. There was an extremely substantial risk that I would miscarry.

My mother and I were in the hospital two weeks before we were released. I was so thankful that my mother was going to be all right. We still had no idea if I would carry the baby full term. *"For with God nothing shall be impossible." Luke 1:37 KJV.* There was too much fluid built up around the fetus that the doctors did not want to make any promises. I was released from the hospital on crutches and on bed rest. I needed to take it easy, follow up with the doctor, so they could watch the baby progress. *"For we walk by faith, not by sight {living our lives in a manner consistent with our confident belief in God's promises}" 2 Corinthians 5:7 AMP.*

I was thirty-seven weeks pregnant when I gave birth to a baby boy. He was born with a full head of black hair, very lite skin and was born with cleft lip and cleft palate. It is where his lips and the roof of his mouth did not completely develop during pregnancy. I was thankful that my son was born but devastated with the new challenges I had to come to accept. He was the most precious thing in the world.

It just seemed as if God was punishing me. I still did not understand why. My oldest son had mental disabilities that I found out at age four and now my second son was born with a birth defect. I knew there was a God, but I did not really believe. I had little faith; I did not understand as to why all these trials were coming into my life. There is a difference in knowing God exist and really believing.

I focused so much on the negative things around me that I did not see the positive side of things. I was blessed that my son was born, alive and well. I struggled with every obstacle that came my way. It was so much for one person to process. I fought every battle on my own, asking nothing from no-one. Looking back, I can see now that I was never alone. All those challenges, I would not have gotten through them without God's help. He was by my side at every moment even when I didn't know it.

God was with me for every struggle, every storm, every obstacle. God was there just waiting for me. He was waiting for me to turn my life to him. To trust in him, with everything in my life. I was blind and did not see. Storms come into our lives that God allows. We do not fully understand the reasons behind some trials or challenges we encounter. God wants us to reach for him to give us strength. God wants us to open our eyes, to see. He wants us to believe in him and to show others what God can do in our lives.

Chapter 8

My mother moved back to Kansas City, and I stayed in Moberly. I was a mother of three children now and I was alone. I had my friends, but they did not have children like me. Damon and I got divorced but he still came to see the kids as often as he could. Although I was pursuing my education, it appeared that completing it would be an unreachable goal. I was so busy taking care of three kids, there was no time for much anything else.

I tried studying for my GED several times. The study books were just too hard. I did not understand most of it and I had no one to help me. Every time I got distracted trying to study, the more frustrated I got. I started to get angry that I was facing all those challenges on my own. I blamed my mother for how my life turned out. I blamed my father for not being there to protect me when I was a little girl. If only my parents had cared. If my mother had not let me be sexually assaulted. I kept placing the blame on others.

What happened to me did not help, but I had a choice. I was twenty years old now, I was an adult. I chose to have those children, and it was my responsibility to care for them. I had to figure it out and quit placing the blame on others. Did I do that? No, I just fought harder and harder so that soon our lives would change. I kept holding on to that little faith, but I continued to live my life in chaos and disaster. *"Come to me, all who are weary and burdened, and I will give you rest." Take my yoke upon you and learn from me, for I am gentle and humble in heart, and you will find rest in your souls. For my yoke is easy and my burden is light." Matthew 11:28-30 NIV.*

We may face hardships and storms because of all the brokenness in this world. God wants us to reach to him in those times, in all situations. Always giving thanks for all the blessings, he brings into our lives. He wants us to have love, hope, and peace through all circumstances. *"Pray continually, give thanks in all circumstances, for this is God's will for you in Christ Jesus." 1 Thessalonians 5:17-18 NIV.*

Even during those times, when we doubt his love for us. Remember, God gave his only son so we could live. Now let's think about that for a moment. He did not want all the hate in this world. Even though we do not understand why we are going through the trials in our lives. God will give you the guidance, and the strength to pull you through it all.

I got tired of being alone, so I moved back to Kansas City. I wanted to be closer to my family. This time I moved to Grandview, Missouri. I moved to a little two-bedroom apartment that used to be an old air force base. I had moved my kids from one situation to another, one home to another. Our lives were like a tornado going through towns moving seventy-five miles per hour. It was turning, twisting, and spinning. It was me that was creating it. I carried that hurt around so much that I just kept disrupting my own children's lives. I dated here and there after the divorce. I really did not have time for anyone in my life.

We would take trips occasionally to see my father in Texas. I remember one time, I rode a Greyhound bus from Kansas City to San Antonio, Texas with three children. That was not a fun ride. I was so excited to see my father. I wanted to make sure we looked nice when we arrived. I was not thinking about the effects of wearing white pants with three small children on the bus. It was a long, uncomfortable ride from Kansas City to Texas. It took about two days before our arrival. By the time we got there, my white pants were no longer white. They were now black. I had to hold my youngest son on my lap for the whole ride. I am trying to add a little humor to this story.

Even though my father had his judgments about my life, I was glad he was a part of it. He hated that I was a young single mother. My parents were disappointed with me. Could I blame them? No, but I did. *"The father of the righteous will greatly rejoice, and he who sires a wise child will have joy in him." Proverbs 23:24 AMP.*

I felt like they had no right to judge me because my life could have been so much different. This was all their fault, not mine. That is how I felt for many years. Regardless of my situation, I needed my parents' support, love, and direction.

I never told my father what had happened to us. My sister had finally told him during a conversation about me. My father made his comments, his judgements about me being a young mother. He talked badly about each one of his children. Never once did he ever ask himself why all of us were screwed up. He had no guilt in leaving us, not one. It did not seem that way. He would cut me out of his life anytime I did something which he did not approve of.

My father and I did not have the best relationship for the first ten years. I held on to that anger for so long. He was never around; he did not seem to love me. He did buy me and my children's things but later he denigrated me. He was a cheater; he did not have the right to judge me for my past mistakes. Do I regret having children at an early age? I did, until God healed me. Do I wish I had made better choices, absolutely! All things come together for good. My children helped me to keep pushing to be a better parent than my own. *"Now I am ready to visit you for the third time, and I will not be a burden to you, because what I want is not your possessions but you. After all, children should not have to save up for their parents, but parents for their children." 2 Corinthians 12:14 NIV.*

I trusted far too many people, believed everything people told me. I was so desperate for love that I was seeking love in all the wrong places. There are things in my life that I will never forget, and people I had to forgive. Throughout my journey, it has aided me in cultivating relationships, and I have consistently been a forgiving individual. The more that happened in my life, the harder it got. The more I wanted to shut people out. *"Put not your trust in princes, nor in the son of man, in whom there is no help." Psalm 146:3 NIV.*

I had always had a kind heart, too kind sometimes. There are people in this world that have unpleasant hearts and all we can do is pray for them. I trusted someone to babysit my children while I went to work, that I shouldn't have. I am not going to go into a lot of details about it. However, I trusted someone, that brutally beat my son to death. He died from a blow to his brain, and liver lacerations. It is still something that is extremely hard to talk about or even write about. It has been twenty-seven years now, and that pain still hurts me more than anything else that has happened in my life.

This was one situation that I just couldn't forgive. It was extremely difficult. How could someone do such a thing to a child, a baby? Why did God allow this to happen? My son didn't deserve to die! I have thought about that moment so many times in my life. I always felt that because of this horrific decision, I could never trust anyone again. I wanted revenge for so many years. *"Do not take revenge, my dear friends, but leave room for God's wrath, for it is written: "It is mine to avenge; I will repay," says the Lord" Romans 12:19 NIV.*

God doesn't tell us we have to forgive everyone when they have no remorse and continue to repeat the injurious behavior. My depression got worse after this. I blamed myself for making the wrong decision trusting the wrong person. The pain my son went through at that moment when his life was taken, I can't even imagine. Just the thought of it tears me up inside. I will never see him grow, all because someone took that from me. This person denied everything, placing blame on a four-year-old or whomever else. *"So, watch yourselves. "If your brother or sister sins against you, rebuke them; and if they repent, forgive them." Luke 17:3 NIV.*

There were stories about what had happened, and everyone had their own version. There were people who believed and said what they wanted. They had no idea, the pain and suffering my family was going through. I was a single mother out there in the world trying to make it on my own. I had no help from the fathers, they

truly trusted someone since then. I was more careful about who I trusted with my children, that even took years. There is a part of my heart that is still hurting deeply from the mistake I made. God is still working to heal my heart. I must read the word, stay in the presence of God. Rinse and Repeat.

There are still times when I feel so weak, times I feel I cannot breathe, times I feel I do not deserve to be living. I lost the relationship with my sister that I had. She just could not let the past go. She continues to hold onto all the traumas we have experienced in our lives. At that moment in my life, I hated everyone that ever hurt me, betrayed me, used me, abused me. There was no way I could ever forgive anyone for any of this. I never really knew exactly what happened that day or the truth about it. I rely on the facts; justice was served and now I must move forward. There was a theory that someone else was involved.

Judgement Day is coming and whomever was involved will be punished, says the Lord. If they do not repent, and ask God for forgiveness, they shall perish. God has directed me on a new path, he is working on my heart, mind, body, spirit, and soul. He wanted me to forgive, it is not my job to hold on to that hatred, anger, resentment, bitterness any longer. The day my son died, I had completely lost all faith in humanity, in God. How could he let this happen? Why didn't God save my son? Was this another punishment from God? I always kept wondering what I did that was so bad to deserve all this. I was thrown at every storm you could have ever imagined for one person. *"Praise be to the God and Father of our Lord Jesus Christ, the Father of compassion and the God of all comfort, who comforts us in all our troubles, so that we can comfort those in any trouble with the comfort we ourselves receive from God." 2 Corinthians 1:3-4NIV.*

My mother said God doesn't give you more than you can handle, but how much did God think I could handle? I did not believe her because I was barely hanging on. There were days I did not know how I had the strength to keep going, to keep fighting, to keep trying. The only way was through God, there is no other explanation of how I survived all of this. He gave me everything I needed to be strong for my living children. *"Let us then approach God's throne of grace with confidence, so that we may receive mercy and find grace to help us in our time of need."* Hebrews 4:16 NIV. My mind was a battlefield that I just could not escape.

The bible provides healing to our body, soul, and spirit. My favorite bible is by Joyce Meyers, The Battlefield of the Mind. Her books have helped me so much in my healing. When we are faced with challenges in our lives, there are times when we feel alone. We are too afraid to talk to others about what we are feeling, what we are dealing with, and are ashamed of what others will think of us. I have read so many Christian books over the last twelve years. There are more people in this world that can relate to your story. I have also learned your story is not for everyone, but you are not alone.

God has healed me in so many ways and has blessed me with more than I deserve. He saw how hard I worked, how determined I was to make a good life for my family. I was delayed several times, pushed back, and got into bad relationships. I have dealt with abuse and everyone I know dealt with alcoholism. This continued throughout my life, which was one thing I had trouble escaping. *"Is anyone among trouble? Let them pray. Is anyone happy? Let them sing songs of praise."* James 5:13 NIV. You need God's help to turn from that darkness to see the light.

I like writing, it is how I have expressed my feelings, it was a way I could talk without talking to someone. I used to write in a journal, of what I was feeling, and I love to write poetry. Here is one that I wrote recently. My first ex-husband came back into my life after twenty-seven years. I could still feel that strong connection between us, but the past remains. We are trying to be friends; it is a work in progress. I still have trouble forgiving myself for the tragedy of our son.

WHISPERS

Sometimes words set triggers that do not escape my mind.
You may not realize how many scars remain.
Fighting battles that cannot escape my mind.
Memories that tear me up inside
A young mother left alone, to fight the battles on her own.
I hear those whispers; it is time to let it go.
God forgives me for the mistakes I made.
Memories that left scars that will always remain.
Those whispers continue to play battles in my mind.
You do not understand, whispers, judgements, all leave scars.
God saved me from the battles that went through my mind.
Each day I fight those battles with God by my side.
No matter what they all say, I am worthy of love.
By the Grace of God, who will forever love me,
no matter what I have done!

Chapter 9

After my son's death, my other two children were taken into custody. My life felt so empty. I worked two jobs and tried to stay busy as much as I could. The busier I was, the less time I had to think about everything else that was going on around me. Six months later, I was reunited with my children, who finally came home. My son Alex went to school, and my daughter Nicki went to a licensed day care center during the day, while I worked. We were trying to get our lives back on track.

I fought for several months trying to prove that I was a good mother. I went to counseling, parenting classes, and every other class the social services made me do. They tried so hard to keep my children away from me, even the wives of the kid's fathers. They all made me pay the price for the mistake I had made. There were times that I almost gave up fighting. I held on to that guilt, and a part of me still does. I made a mistake trusting someone that I never should have trusted with my children. *"Whoever conceals their sins does not prosper, but the one who confesses and renounces them finds mercy." Proverbs 28:13 NIV.*

I did not have to admit my mistakes to the ones who criticized me or defiled me. If I admitted my mistakes to God, he would give me another chance. God would give me a fresh start and provide me with more opportunities. God has provided so much in my life that I never really fully took in. I look around me today and I am in awe. Everything good in my life was because God provided for me. Even when I tried to give up, God would not let me. *"I consider that our present sufferings are not worth comparing with the glory that will be revealed to us." Romans 8:18 NIV.*

I can still remember how I felt, the thoughts that went through my mind, the things people said, the way other people made me feel. They all looked at the mistake I had made but never once stopped to look in the mirror and ask themselves what part they played in all of it. I was a single mother out there raising three children on my own. Their fathers were out there doing who knows what. I cannot expect others to see the real truth. God knows the truth and he is all I need to help me grow, heal, and be renewed.

I know that God sees my pain. Every time I feel that guilt, self-worth, the pain, God is always there to remind me that he is near. I have dealt with so much trauma over the years, and it has been hard to recover from it. I could not heal from it on my own, I needed God. The loss of my child was so massive that it crushed me. *"So, with you: Now is your time of grief, but I will see you again and you will rejoice, and no one will take away your joy." John 16:22 NIV.* It caused a lot of damage in other relationships with people, my husbands, my children. I held on to that hurt for so long that I tried so hard to keep people at arm's length.

People are going to think and say things that are out of our control. Sometimes we allow those thoughts, words, other people's actions to take control of our emotions, how we feel about ourselves. Trust me, the enemy knows your weakness and he will do everything in his power to pull you down. What people think about me is none of my business. I remember a wise woman saying that phrase one night in women's group. It has stuck with me like glue ever since. I must consistently remind myself that I cannot control what other people think about me. I can only control my own mind, my own actions, and how I will continue with my life. I will not let others dictate who I am, I will believe what the Lord says about me. *"In their hearts humans plan their course, but the Lord establishes their steps." Proverbs 16:9 NIV.*

I have been told that I am a very defensive person. I have always felt like I had to protect myself from others. Their harsh words, kicking me to the curb whenever I said or did something they did not like, or talking bad about me. I am not sure what they mean exactly, except that I always seem to explain why I do or do not do something. *"But in your hearts honor Christ the Lord as holy, always being prepared to make a defense to anyone who asks you for a reason for the hope that is in you; yet do it with gentleness and respect." 1 Peter 3:15 NIV.*

I had so many appointments that I had to attend. I had to prove I was a good mother, there was counseling, family counseling, speech therapy for Alex, and play therapy for Nickki. It got to the point I could not hold down a job. I got assistance and worked through each appointment. I wanted my children with me. I was certain of that; never again would I doubt if I were a good enough mother for them. *"But when you ask, you must believe and not doubt, because the one who doubts is like a wave of the sea, blown and tossed by the wind." James 1:6 NIV.* I was not the best mother by any means. I was young and inexperienced. I made the wrong choices and trusted the wrong people. However, that was going to change. There was no one that was as important to me as my children.

I could not date anyone and had to be extremely careful about anyone I came in contact with. The court ordered that anyone that came around my children had to have a background check for any violent crimes. If they had anything negative on their background they could not be around my children. They even taught me how to investigate people so I could be more alert. This went on for over a year. I did everything I could to prove my worth of being a good mother. It was going to be me and my children fighting against the world. No-one and I mean no-one would ever tear my family apart like that again.

A little over a year later, I met a pretty decent guy. He was my first true love. I was still involved with social services, but he did everything they asked. He had a tragic childhood too, so he could relate to what I was going through. My life turned completely around being with him. We were so in love. I was happier than I had ever been. *"You will show me the path of life; In Your presence is fullness of joy; In Your right hand there are pleasures forevermore." Psalm 16:11 AMP.* It was a miracle; a blessing that this amazing man came into my life. He was six feet two inches tall, dark-brown hair, strong, muscular, sexy, and so dang gorgeous. He was a good man.

We spent thirteen years together; we had good and tough times. It was the longest relationship I had ever been in. He helped me raise my children, and I will always be grateful to him for that. I will give thanks to you, Lord, with all my heart; *"I will tell of all your wonderful deeds." Psalm 9:16 NIV.* He gave me a life that I had only dreamed about. He was my partner, everything we had, we worked together to achieve. He was an amazing man that gave me a great life.

Ryan and I met April twenty-four nineteen ninety-eight. We spent all our free time together. He was good to my children, and they loved him. He participated in every family counselling session we had. There were times he would stay over at my house and write me love letters while I was at work. He would write about all the things he wanted to provide for us, how much he loved us, and how he wanted to be a good man for me. I worked at a motel as a housekeeper, and he worked at a lumber company. He really showed me he loved me, and he wanted so much more for us as a family. He was such a kind, strong, loving, generous man.

We had only been together for a couple of months before it was my twenty third birthday. He was going to take me out for a nice dinner. He had also bought me this fourteen-karat gold tweedy necklace. It was my lucky charm for several years. It was so beautiful; he searched everywhere looking for that charm because he knew how much I liked tweedy. He completely understood me, accepted me for all my flaws, accepted my children, and he absolutely loved me. Ryan was the man I had been looking for; he was everything I wanted in a man. *"May He grant you your heart's desire And fulfill all your plans." Psalm 20:4 AMP.*

I was so giddy; I had to look stunning. He was taking me out to dinner to celebrate my birthday. He made me feel so special. I had this wonderful man who adored me and loved me. As I was in the bathroom getting ready, something on the floor was very slippery, that caused me to slip and fall. Of course, at that moment I had no idea that I was pregnant. After the fall, I was fine, so I did not think anything about it. We continued to go out to dinner and had a wonderful evening.

After my car accident, I was not supposed to get pregnant again. I told Ryan that there was little possibility that I could ever have another child. He seemed to be all right with it. I had prayed, and prayed God would give me another chance to have another child. *"Therefore, I tell you, whatever you ask in prayer, believe that you have received it, and it will be yours" Mark 11:24 NIV.*

Two days after my birthday I found out I was pregnant. I was at my sister's house, she stood right beside me, holding my hand. I got one of those home pregnancy tests. I was hoping I was, but I was also scared. I was not sure how Ryan felt about having a baby. Especially, after what I told him what the doctors told me. I was so nervous that I just sat there waiting until I got the courage to talk to him. I wanted another child, but I was afraid of raising another child on my own.

Throughout my life, I have always been afraid to take chances, afraid to trust anyone, afraid of what others thought of me, afraid to love, afraid no one could love me. I needed to ask God for peace. Do not be afraid because our LORD and savior is right by you, no matter where you are or what you are doing, he loves you, *"I sought the Lord, and he answered me; he delivered me from all my fears." Psalms 34:4 NIV.* Believe this and it will be given to you. God is my savior, he truly and completely has delivered me from my way of thinking, my old ways, and my old habits.

When I finally got the nerve to tell Ryan, he was so excited and happy that we were going to have a baby. God had answered my prayers; he was going to bless me with another child. I would do everything in my power to protect this child. A day later, my stomach started cramping, and there was bleeding. Ryan rushed me to the hospital, so that the doctors could examine me. We waited for hours before anyone checked me in. By the time the doctors called me back, I had already had a miscarriage. *"Rejoicing*

in hope; patient in tribulation; continuing instant in prayer."
Romans 12:12 NIV.

We were so devastated; we lost our baby. The doctors wanted me to do a D&C. It is a procedure to have the baby removed from the uterus. I refused to let them do anything. I had waited hours for the doctor to see me. I felt if they had checked on me sooner that I would not have miscarried. However, that was not the case. I was only a few weeks pregnant so no matter what they did there was no saving the pregnancy. I did not understand why God blessed me with another child only to take it away.

In October nineteen ninety-eight, I got pregnant again. *"I prayed for this child, and the Lord has granted me what I asked of him." 1 Samuel 1:27 NIV.* Ryan and I did not want to take any chances that I would miscarry again. He wanted me to quit my job, and he would provide for us. He got a job starting as a union roofer, but it was not the kind of work he really wanted to do. So, he switched to union carpentry. When I had the car accident, the doctors said if I had ever gotten pregnant again, the likely I would carry was a low probability. We had a fifty percent chance that I could carry the baby full term. Since, I already had a miscarriage. We wanted to try and do everything we needed to, so that we had more chances to have this child.

I quit my job and became a stay-at-home mom. I got Alex off to school and stayed home with Nikki. This pregnancy was a miracle, we could not wait to bless our lives with another child. *"The blessing of the Lord brings {true} riches, And He adds no sorrow to it {for it comes as a blessing from God}."Proverbs 10:22 AMP.* The further along I got, the risk decreased. We were in fact going to have a child. I was getting so excited to be a mom again. God had answered my prayers, blessing me with this child. I was going to do everything in my power to love and protect my children.

Ryan was an apprentice through the union. His goal was to become a journeyman so he could provide a good life for all of us. He was so excited about being a father. We were really happy together. We were so excited about having a child together and hoped she would become a part of our lives. I finally had a family that I so longed for all those years. I had a good partner. He loved me so much and always showed it through his words and his actions. He never made me question anything about our relationship!

My pregnancy was going pretty smoothly, the doctors said everything looked good. Ryan and I started to get really excited about our daughter being born. My due date was July twelfth nineteen ninety-nine. It was three days before my twenty-fourth birthday. This was the one pregnancy I gained a lot of weight. I gained forty-one pounds, I only weighed one twenty before I got pregnant. It was a sizzling summer that year, and I could not handle being pregnant any longer.

Ryan sister's suggested that I take this home remedy recipe to induce my labor. That was an awful idea. I cannot remember exactly all the ingredients that were in it, but I do remember castor oil was part of it. You can only imagine what happened. If you know anything about castor oil, well it makes you use the restroom. That is how it induces labor, I gather. I was in labor for twenty-three long hours and had complications. I had complete back labor again with this birth.

I should not have tried to rush the birth of our daughter. I needed to have patience. I took things into my own control. God will direct our steps if we allow him too. Sometimes, we get so impatient waiting for the Lord to answer, for things in life to go our way. We take actions into our own hands and create more disasters. Be patient and wait upon the Lord. *"Be still before the Lord and wait patiently for him; do not fret when people succeed in their ways, when they carry out their wicked schemes." Psalm 37:7 NIV.* Waiting might seem acquiescent; it is actually an act of faith. We should remain focused on God and seek his guidance through prayer and reflection.

When our daughter was born, she was so precious, so small, I had another baby girl that was born with a full head of black hair and lite colored skin. She was seven pounds, eight ounces and nineteen inches long. Madelyn was so beautiful; I just could not let her go. She was this miracle that I prayed for since I had lost my son. *"This is the confidence we have in approaching God: that if we ask anything according to his will, he hears us."* 1 John 5:14 NIV. After one lost child and one miscarriage, here she was. She was my miracle baby. I wanted her to have everything she ever wanted, needed, desired. This was the life I had always dreamed.

Prayer-

Dear Heavenly Father,

Thank you for bringing this beautiful little girl into our life's. Thank you for giving me grace even when I did not deserve it. Thank you for forgiving me for my poor choices. I will do everything I can to protect these children with all my might. In Jesus Name I pray. Amen.

Ryan was with me the entire delivery; he never left my side. He stayed at the hospital and held my hand during the entire labor. This was the first time out of all my children, the father was right by my side. Was this what it felt like to be loved, to have someone care for you so deeply? My life was perfect in that moment. I had my children, a good man, a beautiful and precious family. God blessed me with this wonderful family. *"Take delight in the Lord, and he will give you the desires of your heart."* Psalms 37:4 NIV.

We need God in every part of our lives. Praying during tribulations, giving thanks in everything. *"In every situation {no matter what the circumstances} be thankful and continually give thanks to God; for this is the will of God for you in Christ Jesus."* 1 Thessalonians 5:18 NIV. We have all these things because of God. He provides for us in more ways than we choose to realize. Each day God gives us another breath is another day we can make a change, another day to make a difference in someone else's life, another day to forgive, another day to love, another day to change our ways, another day to rebuild those relationships, another day to ask God for forgiveness, another day to turn our way to God, another day to ask God to change our path, another day to follow God, another day to allow God to direct our paths, another day to pray.

Sometimes during tribulations, it is hard to see what God is doing in our lives. We focus so much on the negative than the positive. We all go through storms, there is no way of getting around that. It is how we manage it that is effective. When we ask God to direct our paths, to renew our minds, it allows us to manage these situations with a clearer mind. When you allow God into your heart, you will know when he is telling you what is right, and what is not right. *"To do what is right and just is more acceptable to the Lord than sacrifice."* Proverbs 23:3 NIV. Be careful though because the enemy likes to play tricks on our mind.

When we try and control our own lives, making our own decisions, without the guidance from God. Our lives become a train wreck. Imagine a train going at a hundred and fifty miles per hour. That train will not stay on track. My life always seemed to be a train wreck. Thinking about those events that happened in my life. How do I write about God's forgiveness, grace, and love in each of these situations. The things in my life was far from being easy, those tribulations caused a lot of pain, but God is showing me exactly what he was doing during those times. I just failed to see all the good he was doing. I was more focused on the bad than the good. It amazes me how God is giving me the words to show others God's grace, forgiveness, and his love.

Chapter 10

It was Christmas nineteen ninety-nine, my father had planned to visit for the Christmas holidays. We had been trying to rebuild our relationship for the past three years via telephone. He called me a few days before he was to visit. He wanted to talk to me about my mother, he told me he still loved her after all these years. He said she was his first love and wanted to know how mom felt about him. It had been twenty years since they had divorced. He told me he had tried finding us but was never successful.

When my father arrived, it was wonderful and exciting to see him again. I was filled with so much joy, happiness, and tears. *"May the God of hope fill you with all joy and peace as you trust in him, so that you may overflow with hope by the power of the Holy Spirit." Romans 15:13 NIV.* We laughed, we talked, we all shared stories, and talked about past memories of my childhood. My father talked about his regrets, how he had missed us and how much he loved my mother. He really had everyone convinced that he really did love my mother after twenty years. Now, see I was this gullible girl who believed everything anyone told me. However, it wasn't only me he had fooled.

My father stayed at a motel down the road from where I lived. He stayed for a week until after New Years's Day. We had an absolutely magnificent Christmas together. He spent time with my children, they all went bike riding. My father was so determined he could still ride a bike at his age. We were all so happy at that moment. It was astonishing to spend the holidays with both my parents. He took my mother shopping for new clothes, new glasses, just about anything else she wanted or needed. My father had money, and he surely let everyone know that too.

He was kind, loving, warm, and gentle. He even had a bit of humor. He also loved to make people smile. He was so flattering that he persuaded my mother in believing his actions were true. I had even convinced my mother. I really believed him. The way he looked at her, the way he treated her. Could this be, could they actually reunite after twenty years, after everything he had done? I wanted to believe, and to this day I do not regret any of it. Now, my mother may have a different opinion about it. I got to know my father regardless of how he was. How would I have ever known otherwise? There are memories with my father that I will cherish for the rest of my life. Some were not pleasant, but some was wonderful.

There were things my father did that broke my heart, and I really never knew if he really loved me. I heard he was proud of me for how I changed my life around, the things I accomplished. He knew I was a Christian before he passed away. God does not want us to talk bad about other people but instead show others what God has done in our lives. Even though there were things in my life that completely broke me. I am here to tell my story. I hope it will encourage you to seek God, and know that God does love you. Your story is not over. *"Commit to the Lord whatever you do, and he will establish your plans." Proverbs 16:3 NIV.*

When it was time for my father to head back home to Texas, he convinced my mother to go with him. My mother still had passion for him. After the life she had lived, the things she went through, she wanted so much to believe. You want to believe in something good, believe that someone genuinely loves you, cares for you. Someone who wants to make you smile, to make you happy. Be careful because people can and will deceive you. This is exactly what my father was doing. He deceived us all.

We should be honest and considerate of others' feelings, needs, and wishes. We should not deceive others for our own gain. It is better to tell the truth, be honest, and truthful, than to lie. Now, I probably would not have moved to Texas otherwise. However, if my father would have been more honest about it, you never know what Ryan and I would have decided. *"Do not steal. " Do not lie. "'Do not deceive one another." Leviticus 19:11 NIV.* Lying and deceiving someone, all creates destruction.

My father wanted so much for me to move to Texas to be closer to him. He believed that I would never leave Missouri without my mother. That wasn't true, I barely knew my father. I was scared to move that far away. A new state, a new life, with a person I barely knew. Just because he was my father didn't mean I trusted him. I am built now to get to know someone before I trust. Trust has to be earned. I loved my father there was no question about that. He left me, and even though I may have forgiven him for that. Our relationship had to be built on honesty.

My mother was in Texas for about a month before Ryan and I decided to move there. I really wanted to wait longer to see how things were going between my parents. My instinct felt something wasn't right. I didn't know if it was my fear or my instinct trying to warn me. Ryan wanted to make the move now before he got too far into the union. He didn't want to start all over again in the apprentice program. I still wanted to wait a little longer before we packed up the kids and started another life. Although getting divorced parents back together is almost every child's dream.

My family and I, and our dog packed up a U-Haul and moved to Texas. Now let's not forget about the dog. Her name was Budha, I have no idea where Ryan got that name. Anyways, she was a yellow hound dog, but she was a loving animal. She was part of our family, so wherever we went, she went. After everything that happened with my son, this was a chance for us to start a new life, it was a new beginning. *"Though your beginning was insignificant, Yet your end will greatly increase." Job 8:7 AMP.*

I had a dysfunctional family, there is no question about that. If we do not embrace the good along with the bad, what do we have? Focusing on what is behind can destroy you. *"Do not be overcome by evil, but overcome evil with good." Romans 12:21 NIV.* Take those experiences and learn from them. Ask God to guide you on the right path, we have two choices obey or destroy. *"Now it shall be, if you diligently listen to and obey the voice of the Lord your God, being careful to do all of His commandments which I am commanding you today, the Lord your God will set you high above all the nations of the earth. All these blessings will come upon you and overtake you if you pay attention to the voice of the Lord your God." Deuteronomy 28:1-2 AMP.* Every decision we make, every moment we share, every tear we cry, there are lessons learned. Our life is a journey, it is up to us to decide which path we go on. We cannot continue to look in the rear-view mirror and see what is behind. Only look at what is in front of us. The past does not define you only your future.

Each day God gives you another breath is another day to make a difference, another day to forgive, another day to make a change, another day to rebuild those broken relationships, another day to show someone you love them, another day to ask for forgiveness, another day to show someone God's love, another day to help someone. We are all broken in one way or another. God can heal us from all that brokenness, there is no other way. God has the power to change our mind, body, and spirit. Believe in him, and you receive all your hearts desires. *"You were taught, with regard to your former way of life, to put off your old self, which is being corrupted by its deceitful desires; to be made new in the attitude of your minds; and to put on the new self, created to be like God in true righteousness and holiness. "Ephesians 4:22-24 NIV.*

Once we got to Texas, we were going to stay with my father in a town called Bandera, Texas. Bandera was a small town out in the country. It was absolutely beautiful. My father had plenty of room for all of us. He had three bedrooms, two baths, double wide manufactured home. It had an enormous kitchen, spacious living room, and bedrooms. It was absolutely breathtaking. My kids were able to make their rooms as their own. I was about to start a new journey in my life.

My father had everything arranged for my mother to babysit my children while Ryan and I got a job. He was going to help Ryan and I with a home, car, and promised that he would do everything he could to help us build a better life. He said he was going to sell us his mobile home. He was planning to buy him another one.

Everything seemed so perfect, too good to be true. Could any of this be possible or was it a dream? My father told one lie after another.

Prayer-

Dear Heavenly Father,

Thank you for all you do, thank you for bringing my father into my life. Thank you for not doubting me, and never stop loving me. Lord, I ask you to guide me in knowing when I am being deceived, knowing when someone's heart is pure and true. I pray LORD that I am able to recognize danger before I am even tempted. You know what my heart longs for and the enemy too. Please LORD, help me to understand the difference. In Jesus Name I pray. Amen!

My father owned his own business, it was a newspaper company. He had contracts all over Texas anywhere from magazines to newspapers. He had his own warehouse, where he prepared the newspapers that were to be delivered. He would sort them out, stuff coupons in the newspapers and deliver. He made a lot of money, and he showed it. My father wore a black cowboy hat, cowboy boots, black corduroy pants, dress shirts with a pocket, rings on all fingers, and wore a gold necklace. He looked like Mr. T with all the jewelry he wore. People believed he resembled Elvis Presley because of his coal black hair, black side burn, and dark colored skin. I never saw it really until after he passed away. In his younger years, he did resemble Elvis a little.

We had been in Texas a few weeks before my father sold his business. He bought me a car so that we were able to get back and forth to work. He was surprised with the car I picked out. I found a gold 2007 Chevy Cavalier, which is a small car. I have no idea why I picked that small of a car with three children, but I did. I think maybe it was because I was looking for the cheapest car I could. I wasn't used to anyone buying me anything that was expensive, especially my father.

Ryan had his union transferred over to Texas and I got a job working at a restaurant. Ryan took the car to work every day because he worked full-time, and I was only working part-time. A month after we moved to Texas, my father left. He left me and my mother again, he moved to San Antonio. He rented him an apartment with his ex-wife. They had gotten back together, this is when it all unraveled. My father made all these promises, that all ended up in one lie after another *"I will not abandon you like orphans: I will come back to you" John 14:18 NIV.* Why did he request me to move closer if this was his intention?

When he left he told us he would make the mortgage payments on the manufactured home and all we had to do was pay the lot rent. We kept our end of the deal but later we found out that my father wasn't paying the mortgage. His house was about to be foreclosed. Ryan was so angry for what my father had done. Ryan was working the apprentice program in the union to make a better life for us. In Texas, the union was neither highly strong or had very good pay.

Everything my father did for me, he took that and twisted it to make me out to be this poor, ridiculous person that couldn't take care of herself. My life significantly improved after Ryan became a part of it. He was my partner and we both had hopes and dreams. We were certain we was going to have a better life with or without any help. The only reason Ryan even agreed to make that move is because he knew how much it meant to me to have a father. He never said that, but I know that is the only reason.

My father started to try and control my life, he was calling my job checking to see if I went to work. I don't know why he so desperately wanted me to move to Texas. I was losing my father all over again. I started to dislike him for this situation that he was putting us in, my family. The way he was hurting my mother all over again. He was not acting like a father. It felt like he was trying so hard to either control my life or sabotage my life. I never understood it. *"Do not be anxious about anything, but in every situation, by prayer and petition, with thanksgiving, present your requests to God. And the peace of God, which transcends all understanding, will guard your hearts and your minds in Christ Jesus." Philippians 4:6-7 NIV.*

My mother was so upset, she couldn't stand to be there any longer. My sister convinced her to move to Wisconsin, and she could stay with her. Ryan was so angry about all of it, the way my father did us. How my father left like that, all the broken promises. He crushed my heart, we all trusted him. Ryan parents lived in Colorado at the time, and they suggested we move to Colorado. We no longer had any family in Missouri and had nowhere to go. If we were to move again, we were going to need help.

A few months after my mother left, Ryan and I decided to move to Colorado. We were going to stay with his parents and start fresh. I was so afraid that my father was going to disown me if we left. I called him and told him how I felt. I asked him if he we moved to Colorado if he would disown me? He told me, "Why would I do that? I love you!" He seemed to be sincere and promised he wouldn't disown me. That was the last time my father spoke to me for ten years.

Ryan and I packed everything up in a U-Haul and moved again. I drove the car, and Ryan drove the U-Haul with Alex, and our dog. The girls rode with me. Madelyn was cutting teeth and was in so much pain during our travels. We drove through locations that had no radio station and the only music I could listen to was a song by Master P. It was the only thing that calmed Madelyn. Nikki tried to calm her down, but nothing worked except that CD. It was a twelve- and half-hour drive. We stopped every so often, to feed the kids and stretch.

Ryan and I lived in Colorado Springs, Colorado for four years. We lived in the same home during that time. Ryan started again with the apprentice program in the union. I couldn't find a job without a high school diploma. I still didn't have one. One day, I saw a commercial on tv about a program that I could do from home to get my actual high school diploma. I studied for a year and received my diploma and later went to college for two years. I studied Accounting and received an associate's degree.

Prayer-

Dear Heavenly Father,

Thank you for the many trials in my life that have led me up to this point in my life. I owe it all to you. You have known what my heart desired ever since I was a little girl. I wanted to find my father, get an education, have a husband, and a family. You provided everything my heart desired. Even though things didn't turn out the way I hoped. I achieved them all because of you. Thank you for loving me when it felt as if no one else did. In Jesus Name I pray. Amen!

Ryan and I ended up moving back to Missouri. We knew how wrong it was to take my children away from their fathers. The union was also much stronger in Kansas City, which paid more and had better benefits. We were still living in Colorado and were commuting back and forth from Colorado to Kansas City trying to purchase our first home. Our finances were good. We both worked ridiculously hard to make our dreams come true. I was a few months away from graduating college with a two-year degree. "Our past did not define us, only our future."

Ryan and I worked hard to build a great life for the kids. He was making good money in the union. We went to fancy restaurants, he bought us nice clothes, and he would buy me diamonds and rubies. Rubies are my birthstone. He would take the kids out on Mother's Day, my birthday, and Christmas to buy me something for the holidays. He always made sure they had a good Christmas and a good birthday. He showered me with roses, balloons, and teddy bears on certain holidays. He was incredibly good to me financially.

On one occasion, a bouquet of flowers, balloons, and a teddy bear were delivered to me at work as an anniversary gesture. It was unexpected as I had not experienced such a thing before. He always tried to provide for us. Don't get me wrong, there were difficult times as well. There are things I try not to remember because God wants me to focus more on what came out of those relationships more than the bad. Please be vigilant, as negative influences may encourage you to dwell on past unfavorable experiences, potentially leading you astray. Have faith in the LORD, and you will find liberation.

Ryan and I was together for ten years before we got married. When he proposed to me, it was so romantic. He had it all planned out. He got me a beautiful engagement ring, took me on a horse and carriage and was going to propose in a gazebo. He knew it was my dream to get married in one, someday. They had a wedding going on the day he proposed. So, he proposed to me right there in the carriage. It was like a scene from a romantic movie, that we all dream about.

When we got married, we planned everything. We bought my wedding dress, rented his tuxedo, bought a wedding cake, wedding knives, wedding gloves, jewelry, and a garter. I had something new, something old, something borrowed. My dress was so beautiful, it was an Ivory colored dress that came to my ankles, a slim fit that covered my body, and pearls that wrapped around my entire dress. Prior to our wedding, I had my hair styled and visited a tanning salon. It was imperative that my wedding day be flawless. I wore wedding gloves, a veil, and a beautiful pearl choker necklace, with pearl earrings. I absolutely looked beautiful.

We got married at a Bed & Breakfast in Branson. Our room was a honeymoon suite, and it was absolutely gorgeous. It had a king-size bed, and breakfast was served every morning. They had a gazebo, and that is where we got married. I was so nervous and happy at the same time. I was so nervous that my glove got stuck to the butt of my dress walking to the altar. This time I was the lucky woman whose dreams where all coming true.

After we returned from our wedding, we had a reception planned for all our family and friends to attend. I can still remember every detail as if it were yesterday. This was one of the happiest moments in my life. This was the only time in my life that I was actually proposed to. Everything I had dreamed about was happening. It brings tears to my eyes, that we didn't survive together. I'm grateful to have experienced this in my life. It was magnificent and I will always cherish those wonderful memories we shared.

Chapter 11

I graduated from college in October 2004. It was tough but I succeeded. I received eight awards throughout college. There were four awards for Dean's list, for having a 3.5 or higher-grade point average. The other four I received was for President's list, for having a 4.0 grade point average. A 4.0 is the highest you can get. I studied hard but there were also times I almost gave up. My children gave me the courage to keep pushing through.

After we moved back to Missouri from Colorado. I got a full-time job, with benefits. After my ninety-day probation trial, I was eligible for health insurance. The first thing I did was make an appointment with a gynecology doctor. I didn't think there was anything wrong, but it turned out that I had abnormal cells in my cervix. The doctors wanted to run some more tests to be certain. They had a theory that I possibly had cervical cancer. I was only twenty-nine years old.

After the results came back from the biopsy, it was confirmed I had pre-cervical cancer. I was scared. *"The Lord will fight for you; you need only to be still." Exodus 14:14 NIV.* I wanted to know my options and what treatment plans that were available. Ryan was supportive as long as I keep fighting and continued to do the treatments. After all the doctors' appointments, the treatments, and two years later I was still diagnosed with pre-cervical cancer. I decided I didn't want to fight anymore, I wanted another option, the next option was to have a hysterectomy.

Ryan was not happy with my choice, I had no more fight in me. By this point, we were already having marital problems. I didn't want any more children, but he did. It was my body and my choice. I made the choice I was going to have hysterectomy. I wanted to move on with my life. Ryan had talked to his sister about it, for moral support of course. She tried to explain to him that my life should have been more important than having another child.

Ryan was still incredibly supportive, he stayed at the hospital the whole time I was in surgery and after. There were complications during surgery, which caused me to be bruised from my inner thighs down to my knees. The bruise wrapped around from the front to the back of my legs. It was the biggest bruise I had ever seen. There was a vein that was not tied off correctly during surgery. I was in the hospital for two days, home for two days, then back in the hospital for two more days. I ended up having a busted hematoma.

This was my first surgery ever in my life and it was the worst. I was in so much pain. It took several weeks for me to heal and a year to feel normal again. Our bedroom at the time was down in the basement. It hurt to walk much, so Ryan rented a recliner chair and set up the downstairs for me. He wanted me to be comfortable so I could get plenty of rest. Even though he didn't agree with my choice, he still tried to do everything he could to take care of me.

Today, it seems like a distance memory. All the things in life we take for granted. I haven't found a man like him since. However, his alcohol and my depression is what destroyed us. *"No temptation has overtaken you except what is common to mankind." And God is faithful; he will not let you be tempted beyond what you can bear. But when you are tempted, he will also provide a way out so that you can endure it." 1 Corinthians 10:13 NIV. "I waited patiently for the Lord; he turned to me and heard my cry. He lifted me out of the slimy pit, out of the mud and mire; he set my feet on a rock and gave me a firm place to stand.*
He put a new song in my mouth, a hymn of praise to our God. Many will see and fear the Lord and put their trust in him." Psalm 40:1-3 NIV.

Ryan and I was together for thirteen years before we split up. It was right before our third-year wedding anniversary. We were together for ten before we got married. The abuse continued, and he started looking for other woman while we were still married There were things he did that he apparently does not remember, or he just clearly denies it. The decision of having hysterectomy later became a problem. He wanted another child, and I was no longer able to give that to him. I truly loved Ryan. He was the one person I seriously didn't think would ever hurt me.

I was now a single mother of two children again. My son was living on his own by the time Ryan and I had separated. I was still my son's legal guardian because of his disability. Life was not easy but during all my tribulation throughout life. I learned a thing to or two. *"When you pass through the waters, I will be with you; And through the rivers, they will not overwhelm you. When you walk through fire, you will not be scorched, Nor will the flame burn you." Isaiah 43:2 AMP.*

I could do this, I was determined. My past will not define me. I was determined that my children would not live that kind of life. Ryan and I really needed marriage counseling. We both had so much baggage that we carried it to our relationship. We found our ways of healing over time. It has been fourteen years now since we divorced. Those memories will always be a part of me. There are things we cannot change in our lives. As I write my story. The more I write the more I feel the release of all those regrets. I have some pretty good memories along with the bad.

I spent so much energy on the bad memories than the good memories. My heart still aches because these people are no longer a part of my life. However, I will always have the good memories that I will cherish. It is what gives me joy. Looking at how bad things turn out only make me sad, angry, resentful, and bitter. Who wants to be around someone like that? Accept things as they are, and seek God to show you the sunshine, the beauty that lies within our hearts.

This was not the life I had planned. Something had to change. Ryan and I decided on joint custody of Madilyn. It took a few threats, a few arguments but we had finally made an agreement. We tried communicating as much as we could tolerate, until Madilyn was eighteen. Did we see eye to eye on everything? No, far from it. We continued to argue over stupid things and threaten each other with our hateful and unkind words.

Hurt people tend to hurt others. This is what I did, the more Ryan hurt me with his words, threats, abuse the more I wanted to hurt him back. Two wrongs does not make a right. Even when it is hard not to, we should say nothing. *"Do not let any unwholesome talk come out of your mouths, but only what is helpful for building others up according to their needs, that it may benefit those who listen." Ephesian 4:29 NIV.* This is how arguments start, someone always has to get the last word in. Well, that is how I was. If he said hurtful words, I threw some back at him. If we can't say anything nice to each other, its best to say nothing at all. Those words can leave scares for years to come, and they can't be undone.

I worked three jobs to provide for my family. My oldest daughter Nikki took care of Madilyn after school until I got home from work. Madilyn was eleven years old, and Nikki was eighteen. This is when I really started praying. I didn't pray very often but every once in a while. When I left Ryan I was only working part-time as a bookkeeper. We wasn't sure how we would make it on our own.

I applied for a full-time accounting position with a construction company. I prayed God would help with finances, that I would be offered that position, that he would help us get through another storm. I had little faith but at that moment I had nothing else to lose. A few days later I got a call and was offered the position. I ended up working both jobs. A full-time job, a part-time job, and another job assisting a lady with her accounting books once a week. God was answering my prayers.

I was able to provide for my children on my own, with no child support and no assistance. It took many years of arduous work. Even though Ryan and I had our problems, he is one person I want to acknowledge because this would not have been possibly if it wasn't for his support throughout college. I have forgiven him for everything that happened, and I hope one day he can forgive me.

During the mist of my relationship with Ryan. I was so broken from everything that happened to me since the age of four. Everything started to boil. It was like hot water boiling on the stove, it is so hot, you could burn. Well, that was me. I hated the abuse, the alcohol, my past, my mistakes. I took all this in my relationship. I became very depressed that I eventually tried to commit suicide a few times. I was on medication for anxiety and depression.

One day, I just took enough, I felt that everyone was better off without me. I held on to that guilt of losing my son. I believed that because of the abuse it was God's punishment for my bad choices. Once, you allow those words to get into your mind, the enemy grasp ahold of you, fester all those choices, all those hurtful memories. The enemy wants you to believe you're not worthy, so you turn away from God, and follow satins ways. Drop to your knees and seek God for forgiveness. *"Come now, and let us reason together," Says the Lord. "Though your sins are like scarlet, They shall be as white as snow; Though they are red like crimson, They shall be like wool." Isaiah 1:18 AMP.* Worship God, and only God because it is he who will give you eternal life.

My depression started to get a little better after Ryan and I had separated. There were days that I still had a tough time getting past everything. I struggled so hard trying to understand why it seemed as if everyone that ever came into my life would treat me so horribly. I kept continually believing there was something wrong with me. I started to work a lot of hours. I was so determined to continue to provide the kind of lifestyle my children were now accustomed to. This is when I started to bury my issues into work.

I would bury those feelings so deep inside my heart that my heart became steel. I was tough and no one would ever break me again. I started to stand up for myself and stopped letting people push me around. Think about it for a second, if you have this pan with burned grease, it is going to be hard getting it to shine again but it can be done. You are going to need to scrub down many layers to see that shiny surface again. No-one would ever get that close to my heart again. I was certain of that.

There was one person that I got involved with shortly after my divorce. It was built more or less on revenge. A few weeks after Ryan and I separated he got involved with a young girl and moved her into our home. I was so heartbroken when I heard the news of him dating a younger girl and later got her pregnant. I wanted him to fight for us, I wanted him to change. He had moved on therefore, I was going to do the same.

We cannot change people, they have to want to change. We can only change ourselves, our way of thinking, how we react in situations, give it all to God to oversee. Nothing is too big for God. Life decisions are not easy however, with God by your side, he will guide you on the right path. We must first seek God, he will shine on you. He will show you that you are worthy, you are loved. God is the one who brought us into this world, we are created in his image.

There were times I got involved in intimate relationship with men that had no desire of any kind of relationship. *"Flee from sexual immorality. All other sins a person commits are outside the body, but whoever sins sexually, sins against their own body."* *I Corinthians 6:18 NIV.* I felt like all men cared about what their own wants and needs. There was no way I would put my heart out there again to have another man tear my heart apart. My heart was so hardening because I wasn't happy with myself, I couldn't love myself. God does not want this for us, he wants to show us love, peace, comfort, happiness, joy, and provide everything our hearts desires.

If we genuinely want to see all these things. All we have to do is be willing to give over our lives to the Lord. Give all your troubles, burdens, anxiety, depression, finances, relationships, addictions, or whatever it is you may be struggling with over to the Lord, and he will set us free. *"So do not fear, for I am with you; do not be dismayed, for I am your God. I will strengthen you and help you; I will uphold you with my righteous right hand."* *Isaiah 41:10 NIV.*

God will renew your mind, spirit, and soul. *"May God himself, the God of peace, sanctify you through and through. May your whole spirit, soul and body be kept blameless at the coming of our Lord Jesus Christ." 1 Thessalonians 5:23 NIV.* "My past will never define me, only my future" I will believe want the Lord says about me. God loves me and will never forsake me. It is he who gives me strength, courage, hope, peace, love, and comfort.

We sometimes find unhealthy ways to cope with hurt instead of seeking God for guidance and instructions. *"He heals the brokenhearted and binds up their wounds." Psalm 147:3 NIV.* We look to alcohol, drugs, shopping, sex, eating, something just trying to find that void that is missing, to make us feel better. None of these are the answer, it all turns to destruction. God is the only way.

Chapter 12

During the last fifteen years of my father life, we rebuilt our relationship. We spent a lot of time together getting to know each other. We saw each other at least twice a year. He could come to Missouri for one part of the year. My youngest daughter and I go to Texas at least once a year. We ended up having a wonderful relationship together. Whenever I needed advice he was always there. There are still times I want to pick up the phone and call him just so I can hear his voice.

Prayer-

Dear Heavenly Father,

Thank you for being there whenever I needed you most. Thank you for never leaving me nor forsaking me. Thank you for restoring my relationship with my father. I am so thankful, I got those memories with him before his passing of this world. You are the truth, the way and life. In Jesus Name I pray. Amen.

There have been people in my life that abandoned me, hurt me, physically abused me, mentally abused me, undervalued me, took from me, used all my mistakes and my weakness against me. I have been in unhealthy relationships, fought depression, had a child too young, got married to young, fought cervical cancer and lost a child. My point is all our choices come with consequences. We can continue to live our lives by blaming others for our lives or we can change our future. We all have a choice. God is the only way.

Every storm I went through in life, I continued to fail because of my own bad choices. I did not have the best role models in my life, nor did I make the right choices, not without God. I did the best I could with the resources that I had. I have dealt with many challenges. Each storm I went through the harder I fought to make my dreams come true. All along God was right there by my side. *"Take delight in the Lord, and he will give you the desires of your heart." Psalm 37:4 NIV.*

I believed in God, but I had little faith. Every storm I went through the less I believed. I did not go to God in prayer for many situations, or choices I made. I trusted only me. Eventually I grew bitter for every raw deal I was dealt with. I hated everyone, trusted no-one, and eventually pushed everyone out of my life. I focused on the situation at hand and thought harder about my choices.

Whenever I start to fight all those battles in my mind. I look around and think about all the things I have accomplished in my life. There was darkness but there was also light. My life would not be where it is today if it wasn't for GOD. I owe it all to him. For every breath he gives me is another day to make a difference, change old habits, handle storms, build or rebuild healthy relationships, forgive someone, love someone, bless someone, love someone. God gives us all the tools we need to make all these changes, we just have to read the word and believe. Believe in God, and God alone. I am in awe of everything he did for me.

God is my everything, he is the one I trust with everything in my life. I still struggle with trusting people of this world. When it is time to trust the right people, God will let me know. He is now and will always be the one I turn to in any situation. It took me several years to know the difference in actually really trusting in God and trusting God. What do I mean by that? We can trust God with some parts of our life but not all. Once, we trust in God with all our life, the transformation is absolutely beautiful.

A bible verse that holds dear to me *"Trust in the Lord with all your heart and do not lean on your own understanding." Proverbs 3:5 NIV.* There are a lot of things that happened in my life that I do not understand. I am tired of trying to understand it all when it is not for me to understand. I can only control my own actions, my own thoughts, and my own life. My old self has died, I have been reborn through Christ.

When I was thirty-eight years old, I met this man that was so kind, compassionate, loving, and gentle. We would talk for hours about God, now we had some pretty heated conversation about the topic. We shared different beliefs. I believed there was a God, but I just did not understand as to why he allowed me to go through all those storms. Was I worthy of love? Did I deserve all this? My mind was a battlefield, I allowed those negative things to feaster in my mind that caused me to continue to fight depression.

My depression got so bad that I tried to overdose a few times. One time I almost died from all the pills I had taken. I am thankful and blessed that I am here today. Everyone around me refused to acknowledge that it was a cry for help. Everyone, except my sister. She knew something was suspicious by my actions and words. She called the police about the situation, and they sent a police officer and an ambulance to my house. I was sitting in my car in our driveway when the paramedics pulled in behind me. They later said, if they had gotten there a few minutes later, I would have died.

It has been twelve years now and I have not had one suicidal thought. I no longer take medication for my depression.

"The Lord is my shepherd, I lack nothing. He makes me lie down in green pastures, he leads me beside quiet waters, he refreshes my soul. He guides me along the right paths for his name's sake."
Psalm 23:1-3 NIV. It has also been twenty-one years, and I have been cancer free. The person, I mention earlier who talked about God a lot. Well, we ended up dating off and on for six years, then we got married. I believed so much, God sent him to me. I really believed he was the one for me. I had never felt so much love, kindness, compassion, grace from anyone I had ever known. All along he was fighting battles of his own.

I wanted so much to believe that if I were more of a Christian that he would want me. If only I would change my ways, my way of thinking , believed more in God and follow his ways. I believed more in this man's affection towards me than I realized. His story is not mine to tell. However, he had lost faith through some trials of his own. The more I continued to learn about God, and wanted more of God in my life, we started to walk different paths. We eventually got divorced.

I prayed for days, weeks, and months. I continued to pray he would find his way back to the Lord, and God would save our marriage. God does not believe in divorce. So, I could not understand as to why God was not answering my prayers. I waited three years after we separated and still nothing, he continued to live his life down a different path. I pressed in more towards God.

Prayer-

Dear Heavenly Father,
Thank you for the many blessings you provide in our lives. Thank you for all the things you provide for our use. I pray for those that are struggling today. I pray over all their struggles, that they see the light, the love you provide, to turn from their ways and seek you LORD. I pray they find happiness, and joy. In Jesus Name I pray. Amen!

Our divorce left me broken and confused. I became the person I thought he wanted me to be, and he changed. Why? Of course, those negative thoughts started to fester in mind. I once again started fighting battles in my mind. *"For God did not give us a spirit timidity or cowardice or fear, but {He has given us a spirit} of power and of love and of sound judgment and personal discipline {abilities that result in a calm, well-balanced mind and self-control}. 2 Timothy 1:7 AMP.* My pastors, along with my brothers and sisters in Christ, provided unwavering support during my times of distress. They taught me how to love myself, to let go of what was, let go of the past hurts, past trials, and to continue to pray. God is who will gives you strength. He may send people, it may be in someone else voice, a bible verses, a song. Listen for the Lord because he will answer.

I still believe that that man was brought into my life for a reason. Even though I do not understand as to why God did not answer my prayers to save our marriage. It is not for me to understand. I am thankful and blessed that he was a part of my life. It is my aspiration that one day our efforts will be fruitful, and he will rediscover his faith, gain clarity, and return to a virtuous path. He opened the door for me to be saved, I only wish I could do the same for him. I am releasing him to the Lord.

Prayer-

Dear Heavenly, Father,
Thank you for bringing this man into my life. Even though I do not understand why you did not save my marriage. I am thankful he came into my life. He came into my life, which ultimately led me to you. You have saved me from the darkness. I pray LORD that you save him from that darkness that is in his spirit. I am so thankful I am breathing today. You sent people in my life to help guide me on my journey. I love you, you are the one I trust with my life before anyone of this world. In Jesus Name I pray. Amen!

God is who gives me strength, wisdom, courage, love, compassion, and forgiveness. God is my amour, it is he who will help me fight this war. *"Finally, be strong in the Lord and in his mighty power. Put on the full armor of God, so that you can take your stand against the devil's schemes. For our struggle is not against flesh and blood, but against the rulers, against the authorities, against the powers of this dark world and against the spiritual forces of evil in the heavenly realms. Therefore, put on the full armor of God, so that when the day of evil comes, you may be able to stand your ground, and after you have done everything, to stand." Ephesians 6: 10-13. NIV.* The war I fight every day in my mind, I will believe what God says about me. For I was created in the image of God. I no longer trust no man before God. I am trying to be what God wants me to be, and even though I fall short sometimes. Every breath I take, I have another day to try again.

God has delivered me from depression, negative thoughts, toxic relationship, poverty, brokenness. *"Create in me a pure heart, O God, and renew a steadfast spirit within me. Do not cast me from your presence or take your Holy Spirit from me. Restore to me the joy of your salvation and grant me a willing spirit, to sustain me."* *Psalm 51:10-12 NIV.* Without God, I would not be still standing here today to even right this book. While storms are inevitable for everyone, our ability to manage them effectively is what truly makes a difference. For every situation that arises, I reach to God for guidance. He always provides, always loves, always preserves, never leaves you nor forsakes you. *"And so, we know and rely on the love God has for us. God is love. Whoever lives in love lives in God, and God in them."* *1 John 4:16 NIV.* My faith has grown even stronger in the last three years. The moment I stopped stressing about situations that was out of my control and let God oversee it, he always provided. There have been times that have been tough. I did not know how I was going to survive financially but God always provided. I have experienced job losses, but each one resulted in new opportunities.

The less I tried to control every situation, the lighter I felt. There is still one part of me that still rips me up inside. When I lost my son. It tore me up so tremendously when certain people even mentioned him, it makes me want to curl up, cry and hide from the world. Those memories are stored in one side of my brain that I have not completely given to God. I think I have, but a specific trigger might cause a different reaction. I have to continually remind myself to get in the Word of God, rinse, and repeat.

"My past will never define me, only my further." With God, everything is possible, he is who took my shattered dreams and renewed all those hopes and dreams. *"But those who hope in the Lord will renew their strength. They will soar on wings like eagles; they will run and not grow weary, they will walk and not be faint. Isaiah 40:31 NIV.* God's grace has set me free. I pray that my story will help you, maybe you have faced the same path I followed. I hope you find love, strength, and encouragement. I pray, I bless someone else knowing God loves you. He can help you, he is the only way. I will believe what the Lord says about me. I will trust the Lord in all my life and know that is all the love I need. *"But blessed is the one who trusts in the Lord, whose confidence is in him. They will be like a tree planted by the water that sends out its roots by the stream. It does not fear when heat comes; its leaves are always green. It has no worries in a year of drought and never fails to bear fruit." Jeremiah 17:7-8 NIV.*

I absolutely believe that because of what little faith I had. God kept pulling me out of the darkness and into the light. Each storm I went through, I became stronger, fighting through each battle I had to endure. God has blessed me in more ways than I could ever possibly imagine. When I do not even deserve it. *"For I am convinced that neither death nor life, neither angels nor demons, neither the present nor the future, nor any powers, neither height nor depth, nor anything else in all creation, will be able to separate us from the love of God that is in Christ Jesus our Lord."* Romans 8:38-39 *NIV.*

There are still times when storms come into my life. I have to reflect back on these scriptures and remember that it is God who gives me strength. Do not let the enemy make you believe you are not worthy because of your past mistakes. It is a trap. When you are dealing with life storms, get into the word, and press in. Rinse and Repeat. Give thanks and praise to God even in the good times.

God Bless, and know God loves you!

Prayer-

Dear Heavenly Father,

Thank you for the many blessings you provided in my life. I am thankful for everything you have provided for me. Thank you for always loving me, guiding me, directing me, and encouraging me. I Pray that you continue to work on my heart, to show me your ways. To continue to show me patience even when it is hard. I pray that you work on my heart and to help me to rebuilt my relationship with my youngest daughter. I pray that you watch over my children, my grandchildren, and my mother. I pray that you heal the brokenhearted, and give them a new heart. In Jesus name I pray. Amen

TEMPTATIONS

Temptations of this world, the pain from so long ago, in times like these loved ones are gone, stories have been told. Temptations of this world. Fighting a war in my mind, which will not let go.

It is not about where I have been, my story is not over. The Lord has ahold of me. Going to survive, rooted in the Lord and going to thrive. Jesus loves me, he died on the cross so I could be set free. Beautiful and worthy to my Lord, I believe what the Lord says, no more lies to be told. My Lord is greater than anything of this world.

Temptations of this world, the pain from so long ago, in times like these loved ones are gone, stories have been told. Temptations of this world. Fighting a war in my mind, which will not let go.

It is not about where I have been, my story is not over. The Lord has ahold of me. Going to survive, rooted in the Lord and going to thrive. Jesus loves me, he died on the cross so I could be set free. Beautiful and worthy to my Lord, I believe what the Lord says, no more lies to be told. My Lord is greater than anything of this world.

HIGH ON A MOUNTAIN

Standing high on a mountain, reaching high for God to come down and rescue me.
Thinking of what my life had to offer, that passed right on by.
Feeling so lost, afraid, ashamed, all alone. Not knowing which way to go. All the mistakes cannot be undone, forgotten. Is there anyone to trust? Is there love in this world?
Standing high on a mountain, reaching high for God to come down and rescue me. Praying that God to show me the way to love, forgiveness, how to release the burden, the pain I carry inside. To show me how to trust and love this world that has done me wrong. I pray he will show me how to let go, to release the burdens that I carry everywhere I go.
Standing high on a mountain, reaching high to feel God's presence, for it is him who will set me free.
God will never let me fall; he will stand by my side through all my battles. For he is all I need, he is so much than anyone could be. He has shown me love, patience, peace, grace, and why? God loves me and will always be there with me.
He showed me a whole new world and has set me free.